I0120382

Theodore Martens, University of Toronto

The University of Toronto Song Book

Theodore Martens, University of Toronto

The University of Toronto Song Book

ISBN/EAN: 9783337181284

Printed in Europe, USA, Canada, Australia, Japan

Cover: Foto ©Thomas Meinert / pixelio.de

More available books at **www.hansebooks.com**

The UNIVERSITY OF TORONTO SONG * BOOK.

"Forsan et haec olim meminisse juvabit."

TORONTO:
I. SUCKLING & SONS,
PUBLISHERS.

TORONTO:
TIMMS, MOOR & CO., TYPOGRAPHICAL MUSIC PRINTERS,
OXFORD PRESS,
23 ADELAIDE STREET EAST.

NATIONAL ELECTROTYPE & STEREOTYPE CO.,
TORONTO.

Daniel Wilson, LL.D., F.R.S.E.,

PRESIDENT OF

University College.

Nor can the snow that age can shed
Upon thy reverend head,
Quench or allay the noble fire within;
But all that youth can be, thou art.

COWLEY

THE accompanying work, compiled and edited by a Committee of Graduates and Undergraduates of the University of Toronto, is offered to the University public and to the musical world as a comprehensive, and, in many respects, a unique collection of College Songs.

Its design is two-fold,—to meet the requirements of the University College Glee Club, and of the undergraduate body, and to be a suitable collection for use in the drawing-room and around the camp-fire.

All the music in the book has been carefully edited by Mr. Theodore Martens, of whose thorough and painstaking services the Committee desire to make especial mention. Wherever necessary or desirable, songs have been re-harmonized, transposed or arranged for male voices, and—a special feature of the work—nearly all choruses have been arranged with parts suitable for college and general use. Great economy in the disposal of space, and the almost entire use of the short score, have made it possible to include an unusually large number of songs. Among them will of course be found many, original, or peculiar to the University of Toronto, that have never before appeared in any permanent or accessible form. Numerous German songs, for which translations have been specially written, will be particularly serviceable and acceptable. To give added interest to the collection, and greater permanence to its value, a large amount of standard music has been included, while many valuable copyright songs have been purchased, or are used by special permission.

The Committee desire to express their cordial thanks to the President and Faculty, to the Graduates and Undergraduates of the University, and to many others less intimately connected with the College, for the assistance generously afforded them in the prosecution of their work.

For permission to reprint certain copyright songs, the Committee and the Publishers acknowledge their obligations to John Farmer, Esq., Balliol College, Oxford; to Messrs. Chappell & Co., Messrs. Robert Cocks & Co., Mr. Edwin Ashdown, Messrs. Novello, Ewer & Co., and Mr. John Blockley, of London, England; and to Messrs. A. & S. Nordheimer, of Toronto.

The Compilation Committee and the Publishers, Messrs. I. Suckling & Sons, have made every endeavour to discover the authors and owners of all songs in the work. Should any cases have eluded their vigilance, the Publishers ask the kind indulgence of those whose permission would gladly have been sought.

University College,
Toronto, *December, 1887.*

TORONTO UNIVERSITY SONG BOOK.

National and Patriotic.

MAY GOD PRESERVE THEE, CANADA.

Moderato.
R. S. AMBROSE.
1. May God pre-serve thee, Ca - na - da, Tho' child a - mong the
2. Though we may ne - ver read the page, That tells thy deeds of
3. In spring - tide flush, thro' sum - mer's glow When au - tumn winds are
Na - tions, 'Mid proud - est lands, strong hearts and hands Shall claim for thee a
glo - ry, When na - tions now in prime of age, Have with the years grown
sing - ing, In win - ter's snow, through weal and woe, This song shall still be
sta - tion,
hoar - y.
ring - ing.
CHORUS.
Land of the for - est and the lake, Land of the rush - ing
cres.
riv - er, Our prayers shall rise for thy dear sake, For - ev - er and for - ev - er.

After 3rd verse.

God save our gra - cious Queen, Long live our no - ble Queen,
God save the Queen. Send her vic - to - ri - ous, Hap - py and
glo - ri - ous, Long to reign o - ver us, God save the Queen.

GOD PRESERVE OUR NATIVE LAND.

J. DAVENPORT KERRISON.

1. God pre-serve our na - tive land, Fair Can - a - da the free, May
2. Should for - reign foes our land e'er threat With de - so - la - tion fell, God
3. Be pre - sent with our ru - lers, Lord, And all their coun - cils guide; From
His right hand pro - - tect our land, And guard her lib - er - ty.
guard the right and lend us might, Th' in - va - der to re - pel.
knav - ish tricks of pol - i - tics, Turn Thou their hearts a - side.

Then shall each val - ley, each moun - tain and plain,

E - cho in cho - rus The glad re - - frain—

Can - a - da, fair Can - a - da, God's bles - sing rest on thee; May

His right hand pro - tect our land And guard her lib - er - ty.

CANADA, THE GEM IN THE CROWN.

Words by J. DAVIDS. Music by F. H. TORRINGTON.

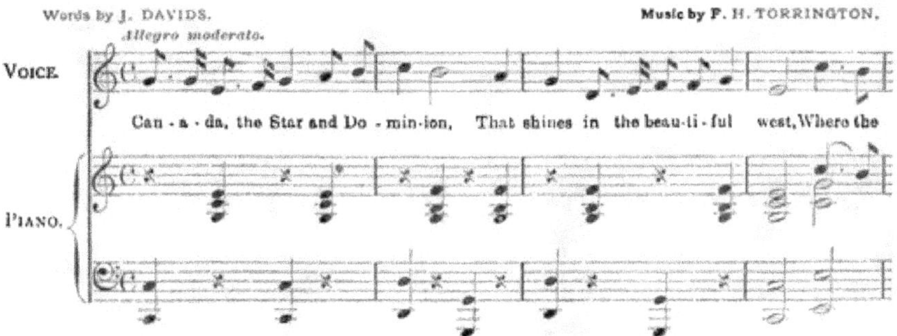
Allegro moderato.
VOICE.
PIANO.
Can - a - da, the Star and Do - min-ion, That shines in the beau-ti-ful west, Where the

cresc.
dim.
p
Sun in a robe of ver - mil - lion, Sinks soft - ly and sweet - ly to rest, The
cresc.
dim.
land of a great fed - er - a - tion, Which time will nev-er un - tie, Till it
sf
cresc.
sf
mf
swell to a glo - ri - ous na - tion, With a char - ter that nothing can buy. Then
con spirito
cresc.
mf
cheer, cheer for Can - a - da, For her sing loud and long, We
cresc.
mf

marcato.
will de-fend dear Can-a-da, In bat-tle and in song.

CHORUS.
TENORS.
Then cheer, cheer for Can-a-da, For her sing loud and
BASSES.
PIANO.
mf
cresc.

FINE.
long. We will de-fend dear Can-a-da In bat-tle.... and in song.
FINE.

un poco moderato.
The Gem in the crown of Bri - tan - nia, The fair-est it ev - er shall
p
be, A cross in the glo - ri-ous ban-ner That floats up-on ev-'ry sea, The
pride of our fathers we'll ev - er De - fend and claim as our own, And we
ad lib.
Dal Segno al Fine
know that old England will nev - er Her Can - a - di - an daughter dis - own. Then
cresc.
Dal Segno al Fine

THE MAPLE LEAF FOR EVER.*

Con spirito.
ALEXANDER MUIR.
PIANO.
1. In days of yore, from Bri - tain's shore, Wolfe the daunt - less
2. At Queens - ton Heights and Lun - dy's Lane, Our brave fa - thers,
3. Our fair Do - min - ion now ex - tends From Cape Race to
4. On mer - ry Eng - land's far-famed land May kind Hea - ven
he - ro came, And plant - ed firm Bri - tan - nia's flag, On Ca-na-da's fair do-
side by side, For free - dom, homes, and loved ones dear, Firmly stood and no - bly
Noot - ka Sound; May peace for e - ver be our lot, And plen-teous store a-
sweet - ly smile; God bless Old Scot - land e - ver - more, And Ire - land's Em - er-ald
main. Here may it wave, our boast, our pride, And joined in love to -
died; And those dear rights which they main-tained, We swear to yield them
bound: And may those ties of love be ours Which dis - cord can - not
Isle! Then swell the song, both loud and long, Till rocks and for - est

* By permission of Messrs. A. & S. NORDHEIMER, Toronto.

geth-er, The This-tle, Sham-rock, Rose en-twine The Ma-ple Leaf for ev-er!
ne-ver! Our watchword ev - er - more shall be, The Ma-ple Leaf for ev-er!
se ver, And flour-ish green o'er Freedom's home, The Ma-ple Leaf for ev-er!
qui-ver, God save our Queen, and Hea - ven bless The Ma-ple Leaf for ev-er!
CHORUS.
1st & 2nd Tenors.
1. The Ma - ple Leaf, our em-blem dear, The Ma - ple Leaf for ev - er! God
2. The Ma - ple Leaf, our em-blem dear, The Ma - ple Leaf for ev - er! God
3. The Ma - ple Leaf, our em-blem dear, The Ma - ple Leaf for ev - er! And
4. The Ma - ple Leaf, our em-blem dear, The Ma - ple Leaf for ev - er! God
Bass.
Piano.
f
save our Queen, and Hea - ven bless The Ma - ple Leaf for ev - er!
save our Queen, and Hea - ven bless The Ma - ple Leaf for ev - er!
flour - ish green o'er Freedom's home, The Ma - ple Leaf for ev - er!
save our Queen, and Hea - ven bless The Ma - ple Leaf for ev - er!

VIVE LA CANADIENNE.

Allegro.

1. Viv - - e la Can - a - - dien - - ne, Vo - le, mon cœur,
2. Nous la men-ons aux no - - - ces, Vo - le, mon cœur,

FINE.

vo - - le, Viv - e la Can - a - - dien - - ne, Et ses jo - lis yeux doux.
vo - - le, Nous la men-ons aux no - - ces, Dans tous ses beaux a - tours.

Solo 1st time. D. C.

Et ses jo lis yeux doux, doux, doux, Et ses jo - lis yeux doux.
Dans tous ses beaux a - tours, tours, tours. Dans tous ses beaux a - tours.

3. Nous faisons bonne chère,
Vole, mon cœur, vole,
Nous faisons bonne chère,
Et nous avons bon goût. (*ter.*)
Chorus—Vive la Canadienne, etc.

4. On danse avec nos blondes,
Vole, mon cœur, vole,
On danse avec nos blondes,
Nous changeons tour à tour. (*ter.*)
Chorus—Vive la Canadienne, etc.

5. Alors toute la terre,
Vole, mon cœur, vole,
Alors toute la terre,
Nous appartient en tout. (*ter.*)
Chorus—Vive la Canadienne, etc.

6. Ainsi le temps se passe,
Vole, mon cœur, vole,
Ainsi le temps se passe,
Il est vraiment bien doux. (*ter.*)
Chorus—Vive la Canadienne, etc.

UN CANADIEN ERRANT.

With feeling. Translated by B. MORTON JONES, '91.

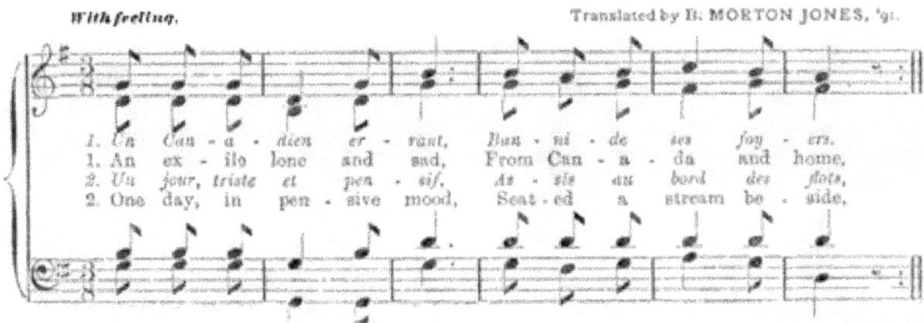
1. Un Can - a - dien er - rant, Ban - ni - de ses foy - ers.
1. An ex - ile lone and sad, From Can - a - da and home,
2. Un jour, triste et pen - sif, As - sis au bord des flots,
2. One day, in pen - sive mood, Seat - ed a stream be - side,

Par - cou - rait en pleu - rant, Des pa - ys é - tran - gers.
By fate, in fo - reign lands, Doom'd ev - er more to roam.
Au cou - rant fu - - gi - tif, Il a - dres - sa ces mots :
To the fast flow - ing wave, Thus, weep - ing low, he cried :
Par - cou - rait en pleu - rant,.... Des pa - ys é - tran - gers.
By fate, in fo - reign lands,... Doom'd ev - er more to roam.
Au cou - rant fu - gi - tif,...... Il a - dres - sa ces mots :
To the fast flow - ing wave,.... Thus, weep - ing low, he cried

3\. "Si tu vois mon pays,
Mon pays malheureux,
Va, dis à mes amis
Que je me souviens d'eux.

4\. "O jours si pleins d'appas
Vous êtes disparus,
Et ma patrie, hélas!
Je ne te verrai plus!

5\. "Plongé dans les malheurs,
Loin de mes chers parents,
Je passe dans les pleurs
D' infortunés moments."

6\. "Non, mais en expirant,
O mon cher Canada!
Mon regard languissant
Vers toi se portera."

3\. "If thou, in onward course,
Should'st see my land, oh then,
Go, tell my friends that I
Mindful of them remain.

4\. "Oh hours so full of joy,
Fled with the years long o'er,
And thee, my native land,
I shall behold no more.

5\. "Plunged in the depths of woe,
No friend to soothe appears;
The moments as they pass,
Bring only sighs and tears."

6\. "When low within my breast,
Life's flick'ring spark shall burn,
To thee, oh Canada,
My dying eye shall turn."

A LA CLAIRE FONTAINE.

Lively.
1. A la clai - re fon - tai - ne, M'en al - lant pro - me - ner, J'ai trou - vé l'eau si bel - le,
2. J'ai trou - vé l'eau si bel - le, Que je m'y suis baig - né, Sous les feuil - les d'un chê - ne
3. Sous le feuil - les d'un chê - ne Je me suis fait sé - cher, Sur la plus hau - te bran - che
4. Sur la plus hau - te bran - che Le ros - sig - nol chan - tait, Chan - te, ros - sig - nol chan - te,

CHORUS.
Que je m'y suis baig-né.
Je me suis fait sé - cher
Le ros - sig - nol chan-tait.
Toi qui as le coeur gai ;
Lui ya longtemps que je t'ai-me, Ja-mais je ne t'oub-lier - ai.

5. Chante, rossignol, chante,
Toi qui as le coeur gai ;
Tu as le coeur à rire,
Moi, je l'ai-t-à pleurer.
Chorus—Lui y a, etc.

6. Tu as le coeur à rire,
Moi, je l' ai-t-à pleurer.
J'ai perdu ma maîtresse,
Sans l' avoir mérité.
Chorus—Lui y a, etc.

7. J'ai perdu ma maîtresse,
Sans l'avoir mérité,
Pour un bouquet de roses,
Que je lui refusai.
Chorus—Lui y a, etc.

8. Pour un bouquet de roses,
Que je lui refusai.
Je voudrais que la rose
Fût encore au rosier.
Chorus—Lui y a, etc.

9. Je voudrais que la rose
Fût encore au rosier,
Et moi et ma maîtresse
Dans les mêm's amitiés,
Chorus—Lui y a, etc.

RULE BRITANNIA.

Maestoso.
Harmonized by THEODORE MARTENS.
1st Tenor.
1. When Bri - tain first...... at Heav'n's com-mand, A - rose............ from out the
2. The na - tions not ...... so blest as thee, Must in .... their turn to
2nd Tenor.
1st Bass.
1. When Bri - tain first...... at Heav'n's com-mand, A - rose .... from out the
2. The na - tions not ...... so blest as thee, Must in ...... their turn to
2nd Bass.
A-rose
Must in
a - - zure main, Arose, arose from out the a - zure main, This was the charter, the
ty - - rants fall, Must in, must in their turn to ty-rants fall, While thou shalt flou-rish, shalt
A - rose.
Must in..
a - - - zure main, Arose, arose from out the a - zure main, This was the charter, the
ty - - - rants fall, Must in, must in their turn to ty-rants fall, While thou shalt flou-rish, shalt

char - ter of the land, And guardian an......gels sang the strain,
flou-rish great and free, The dread and en.........vy of them all,
Rule Bri-tan-nia! Bri-
char - ter of the land, And guardian an......gels sang the strain,
flou-rish great and free, The dread and en.........vy of them all,
Rule Bri-tan-nia! Bri-
f CHORUS.
tan-nia rule the waves, For Bri - tons ne - - - ver shall be slaves. Rule Britannia! Bri-
f
f
tan-nia rule the waves, For Bri - tons ne - - - ver shall be slaves. Rule Britannia! Bri-
f
tan - nia rule the waves, For Bri - tons ne - - - - ver shall be slaves.
tan - nia rule the waves, For Bri - tons ne - - - - ver shall be slaves.

3. Still more majestic shalt thou rise,
More dreadful from each foreign stroke,
As the loud blast, the blast that rends the sky,
Serves but to root thy native oak.
Chorus.—Rule Britannia, etc.

4. The muses still with freedom found,
Shall to thy happy coast repair,
Blest Isle with beauty, with matchless beauty crowned,
And manly hearts to guard the fair.
Chorus.—Rule Britannia, etc.

SCOTS WHA HAE.

Words by BURNS. Arranged for Male Voices by T. M.

1. Scots wha hae wi' Wallace bled, Scots wham Bruce has af - ten led, Wel-come to your gor - y bed, Or to vic - to - ry. Now's the day and now's the hour, See the front of bat tle lour, See ap-proach proud Edward's power, Chain and sla - ve - ry.
2. Wha will be a trai-tor knave? Wha will fill a cow-ard's grave? Wha sae base as be a slave? Let him turn and flee. Wha for Scotland's King and law, Freedom's sword will strongly draw, Free-man stand, or free - man fa', Let him fol-low me.
3. By op-pres-sions, woes and pains, By our sons in ser - vile chains, We will drain our dear - est veins, But they shall be free. Lay the proud u - sur per low, Ty-rants fall in ev - 'ry foe, Lib - er - ty's in ev - 'ry blow, Let us do or die.

THE MINSTREL BOY

Words by MOORE. Arranged by BALFE.

1. The min - strel boy to the war is gone, In the ranks of death you'll find him; His fa - ther's sword he hath gird - ed on, And his wild harp slung be-
2. The min - strel fell, but the foe-man's chain Could not bring that proud soul un - der; The harp he loved ne'er spoke a - gain, For he tore its chords a-

hind him. "Land of song!" said the war - rior bard, "Tho' all the world be-
sun - der, And said, "No chain shall sul - ly thee, Thou soul of love and
trays thee, One sword at least thy rights shall guard, One faith - ful harp.... shall praise thee."
brav - 'ry! Thy songs were made for the pure and free, They shall never sound.. in slav - 'ry."

MARCH OF THE MEN OF HARLECH.

Words by WILLIAM DUTHIE.* Harmonized for Male Voices by T. M.

Tempo marziale.

1. Men of Har-lech! in the hol-low, Do ye hear, like rushing bil-low, Wave on wave that surg-ing fol-low Bat-tle's dis - tant sound?
'Tis the tramp of Sax-on foe-men, Sax-on spearmen, Saxon bowmen,—Be they knights or hinds or yeomen, They shall bite the ground!
Loose the folds a - sun - der, Flag we con-quer un - der! The pla - cid sky, now bright on high, Shall launch its bolts in

2. Rock - y steeps and pass-es nar-row Flash with spear and flight of arrow, Who would think of death or sorrow? Death is glo - ry now!
Hurl the reel-ing horseman ov - er! Let the earth dead foemen cover! Fate of friend, of wife, of lov - er, Trem-bles on a blow!
Strands of life are riv - en; Blow for blow is giv - en In dead-ly lock or bat - tle shock, And mer - - cy shrieks to

*By permission of Messrs. Novello, Ewer & Co., London.

thun-der. On-ward! 'tis our coun-try needs us. He is brav-est, he who leads us!
hea-ven! Men of Har-lech! young or hoar - y, Would you win a name in sto - ry?
Hou - our's self now proud - ly heads us! Cam - bria, God, and Right!
Strike for home, for life, for glor - y! Cam - bria, God, and Right!

HAIL COLUMBIA.

Words by JUDGE HOPKINSON, 1798. PROF. PHYLO, 1789.

With Energy.

1. Hail Co-lum - bia, hap - py land! Hail, ye heroes, heav'n-born band, Who fought and bled in
2. Immortal patriots, rise once more, Defend your rights, defend your shore! Let no rude foe, with
3. Behold the chief who now commands, Once more to serve his country stands The rock on which the

freedom's cause, Who fought and bled in freedom's cause, And when the storm of war was gone, En-
im - pious hand, Let no rude foe, with im pious hand, In-vade the shrine where sacred lies Of
storm will beat, The rock on which the storm will beat, But armed in vir - tue, firm and true, His

joy'd the peace your val - or won. Let in - de-pen-dence be our boast, Ev - er mind-ful
toil and blood, the well-earn'd prize. While off'ring peace, sincere and just, In Heav'n we place a
hopes are fixed on Heav'n and you. When hope was sinking in dismay, When glooms ob - scur'd Co-

what it cost; Ev - er grate-ful for the prize, Let its al - tar reach the skies.
man - ly trust, That truth and jus - tice will pre - vail, And ev' - ry scheme of bond-age fail.
lum - bia's day, His stead - y mind, from changes free, Re-solved on death or lib - er - ty.
CHORUS.
Firm, u - ni - ted, let us be,..... Ral - ly - ing 'round our lib - er - ty,.......
As a band of broth - ers join'd, Peace and safe - ty we shall find.
LA MARSEILLAISE.
ROUGET DE LISLE, 1792.
Con animo
f
1. Allons, en - fants de la pa - tri - - e, Le jour de gloire est ar - ri - vé. Con - tre
2. Que veut cet - te hor-de d'es-cla - ves, De traî-tres, de rois con - ju - rés! Pour qui
3. Tremblez ty - rans et vous per - fi - des, L'oppro-bre de tous les par - tis! Trem-blez,—
1. Ye sons of France, awake to glo - ry! Hark, hark! what myriads bid you rise! Your children
mf
nous de la tyran - ni - e, L'é-tendard sanglant est le - vé, L'é - ten-dard sang-lant est le-
ces ig - no-bles en - tra-ves, Ces fers, dès longtemps prépa - rés? Ces fers, dès longtemps pré-pa-
vos pro-jets parri - ci-des Vont en - fin re-ce voir leur prix, Vont en - fin re - ce-voir leur
wives, and grand-sires hoar-y: Behold their tears, and hear their cries, Behold their tears and hear their
p
f

ré, En-ten-dez vous dans les cam - pa-gnes Mu-gir ces fé - ro-ces sol - dats? Ils
és! Français! pour nous, ah! quel ou - tra-ge! Quels transports il doit ex - ci - ter! C'est
prix. Tout est sol-dat pour vous com - bat - tre; S'ils tom-bent, nos jeu-nes hé - ros La
cries! Shall hate-ful ty-rants mischief breeding, With hireling hosts, a ruf - fian band, Af-
vien-nent, jus-que dans nos bras, É-gor - ger nos fils, nos com-pa-gnes!
nous qu'on o - se me - na - cer De rendre à l'an - tique es - cla - va - ge.
France en produit de nou-veaux, Con-tre vous tous prêts à se bat-tre.
fright and desolate the land, While peace and liber-ty lie bleeding!
Aux ar - mes, ci-toy-
To arms, to arms, ye
ens! For - mez...... vos ba - tail - lons: Mar - chez, mar - chez!
brave! Th' a - veng - ing sword unsheathe! March on, march on!
qu'un sang im - pur A - breu - - - ve nos sil - lons.
all hearts re - solved On vic - - - to - ry or death.

4. *Français! en guerriers magnanimes,*
Portez ou retenez vos coups;
Épargnez ces tristes victimes,
A regret s'armant contre nous;
Mais le despote sanguinaire,
Mais les complices de Bouillé—
Tous ces tigres qui sans pitié
Déchirent le sein de leur mère.
Aux armes, &c.

5. *Amour sacré de la patrie,*
Conduis, soutiens nos bras vengeurs.
Liberté, Liberté chérie,
Combats avec tes défenseurs;
Sous nos drapeaux que la victoire
Accoure à tes mâles accents,
Que tes ennemis expirants,
Voient ton triomphe et notre gloire.
Aux armes, &c.

2. With luxury and pride surrounded,
The vile, insatiate despots dare,
Their thirst of gold and power unbounded,
To mete and vend the light and air.
Like beasts of burden would they load us—
Like gods would bid their slaves adore—
But man is man—and who is more?
Then shall they longer lash and goad us?
To arms, etc.

3. Oh liberty! can man resign thee,
Once having felt thy generous flame?
Can dungeons, bolts and bars confine thee,
Or whips thy noble spirit tame?
Too long the world has wept, bewailing
That falsehood's dagger tyrants wield—
But freedom is our sword and shield,
And all their arts are unavailing.
To arms, etc.

DIE WACHT AM RHEIN.

Words by MAX SCHNECKENBURGER, 1840. CARL WILHELM, 1854.

Con brio.
1. { Es braust ein Ruf wie Don - ner-hall, Wie Schwertge - klirr und Wo - gen - prall: Zum
{ A voice resounds like thun - der peal, 'Mid dashing wave and clang of steel; "The
2. { Durch Hun - dert-tau - send zuckt es schnell, Und Al - ler Au - gen blit - zen hell; Der
{ They stand a hun-dred thou-sand strong, Quick to a - venge their country's wrong; With
Rhein, zum Rhein, zum deutschen Rhein! Wer will des Stro - mes Hü - ter sein?
Rhine, the Rhine, the German Rhine! Who guards to - day my stream di - vine?"
Deut - sche, bie - der, fromm und stark, Be - schützt die heil' - ge Lan - des - mark.
fil - ial love their bo - soms swell; They'll guard the sa - cred land - mark well.
CHORUS.
Lieb Va - terland! magst ru - hig sein, Lieb Va - terland! magst ru - hig sein; Fest steht und
Dear Fa - therland! no dan - ger thine, Dear Fa-therland! no dan - ger thine; Firm stand thy
treu die Wacht, die Wacht am Rhein! Fest.. steht und treu die Wacht, die Wacht am Rhein!
sons to watch, to watch the Rhine! Firm.. stand thy sons to watch, to watch the Rhine!

3. *So lang' ein Tropfen Blut noch glüht,*
Noch eine Faust den Degen zieht,
Und noch ein Arm die Büchse spannt,
Betritt kein Feind hier deinen Strand.—Chorus.

4. *Der Schwur erschallt, die Woge rinnt,*
Die Fahnen flattern hoch im Wind;
Am Rhein, am Rhein, am deutschen Rhein,
Wir alle wollen Hüter sein!—Chorus.

3. While flows one drop of German blood,
Or sword remains to guard thy flood,
While rifle rests in patriot's hand,
No foe shall tread thy sacred strand!—*Chorus.*

4. Our oath resounds, the river flows,
In golden light our banner glows,
Our hearts will guard thy stream divine,
The Rhine, the Rhine, the German Rhine!—*Cho.*

AUSTRIAN NATIONAL HYMN.

Translation by J. EDMUND JONES, '88.
HAYDN, 1797.
1. Gott er-hal-te Franz den Kai-ser, un-sern gu-ten Kai-ser Franz!
Hoch als Herrscher, hoch als Wei-ser, steht er in des Ruh-mes Glanz!
1. God preserve our no-ble sov'-reign, Franz our Emperor, great and good!
High in coun-cil, high in pow-er, Glor-ious hath he ev-er stood.
Lie-be win-det Lor-beer-rei-ser Ihm zum e-wig grü-nen Kranz!
Gar-lands to keep green his mem'-ry Love en-twines, and ev-er should.
Gott er-hal-te Franz den Kai-ser, un-sern gu-ten Kai-ser Franz!
God preserve our no-ble sov'-reign, Franz, our Emp'ror great and good!

2. Ueber blühende Gefilde reicht sein Scepter weit und breit;
Säulen seines Thron's sind Milde, Biedersinn und Redlichkeit,
Und von seinem Wappenschilde strahlet die Gerechtigkeit.
Gott erhalte, etc.

3. Sich mit Tugenden zu schmücken, achtet er der Sorgen werth.
Nicht, um Völker zu erdrücken, flammt in seiner Hand das Schwert,
Sie zu segnen, zu beglücken, ist der Preis, **den** *er begehrt.*
Gott erhalte, etc.

4. Er zerbrach der Knechtschaft Bande, hob zur Freiheit uns empor!
Früh erleb' er deutscher Lande, deutscher Völker höchsten Flor,
Und vernehme noch am Rande später Gruft der Enkel Chor:
Gott erhalte, etc.

2. Over flourishing dominions
Far and wide his rule extends.
In his dealings with his people
Righteousness with Mercy blends;
And from off his flashing scutcheon
Rays of brightness Justice sends.
God preserve, etc.

3. To adorn his life with virtues
Is his high and steadfast aim.
Not against his loyal people
Doth his sword with terror flame;
To have made them great and powerful
Is the prize that he will claim.
God preserve, etc.

4. Freedom's blessings he hath given us,
Slavery's bonds he burst in twain.
Early may he see his country
To its highest power attain;
And when his last day is ended,
Let this chorus still remain;
God preserve, etc.

RUSSIAN NATIONAL ANTHEM.

Maestoso. Arr. for Male Voices.

Long live our no - ble Czar! God keep him safe, with - in his realm in pow'r and peace to reign, Ev - er vic - to ri - ous...... Of our Faith the cham - pion..... Long live the Czar, Long live the Czar!

College Songs and Choruses.

OLD GRIMES.

Words by A. G. GREENE. Tune,—"AULD LANG SYNE."

1 Old Grimes is dead, that good old man, We ne'er shall see him more; He used to wear a
2 His heart was o-pen as the day, His feel-ings all were true; His hair was some in-
long black coat, All but-toned down be-fore.
clined to gray, He wore it in a queue.
CHORUS.
Old Grimes, old Grimes, old Grimes, old Grimes, old
Grimes, old Grimes, old Grimes, Old Grimes, old Grimes, old Grimes, old Grimes, old Grimes, old Grimes, old Grimes.

3. Whene'er he heard the voice of pain,
His breast with pity burned;
The large round head upon his cane,
From ivory was turned.

4. Kind words he ever had for all,
He knew no base design;
His eyes were dark and rather small,
His nose was aquiline.

5. He lived at peace with all mankind,
In friendship he was true;
His coat had pocket-holes behind,
His pantaloons were blue.

6. Unharmed, the sin which earth pollutes,
He passed securely o'er,
And never wore a pair of boots,
For thirty years or more.

7. But good old Grimes is now at rest,
Nor fears misfortune's frown;
He wore a double-breasted vest,—
The stripes ran up and down.

8. He modest merit sought to find,
And give it its desert,
He had no malice in his mind,
No ruffles on his shirt.

9. His neighbors he did not abuse,
Was sociable and gay,
He wore nor lefts nor rights for shoes,
And changed them every day.

10. His knowledge, hid from public gaze,
He did not bring to view,
He made a noise town-meeting days,
As many people do.

11. Thus, undisturbed by anxious cares,
His peaceful moments ran,
And everybody said he was
A fine old gentleman.

LITORIA.

(TORONTO VERSION.)

Allegretto.
SOLO.
F. C. WADE,
VOICE.
PIANO.
Ye blooming fresh-man dons his gown, Swe - de - le - we - dum bum. And
walks ye earth with awful frown, Swe-de - le - we - dum bum.
DUET.
He sees ye maidens' glances sly,
Swe - de - le - we-tchu - hi - ra - sa, And roll-eth his mag-net - ic eye, Swe - de - le - we - dum bum.
f
CHORUS.
1ST AND 2ND TENOR.
Li - to - ri - a! Li - to - ri - a! Swe - de - le - we - tchu
1ST AND 2ND BASS.

hi - ra - sa, Li - to - ri - a! Li - to - ri - a! Swe - de - le - we - dum bum.

1. Ye blooming freshman dons his gown,
And walks ye earth with awful frown.
He sees ye maidens' glances sly,
And rolleth his magnetic eye.

2. He's brought before ye Mufti's throne,
'Mid sulphurous smoke and muffled groan,
'Mid red-hot brands and boiling tar,
He scenteth danger from afar.

3. Ye spikes cut deep, ye race is run,
He rides ye chariot of ye sun.
Ye brake is put on Ixion's wheel,
L'Inferno's inmost caverns reel.

4. Ye ritual he chanteth now,
Dread Lucifers attend his vow;
Ye sounds die 'way, ye ordeals cease,
"Ad initiandos tirones."

5. As tiniest voice from tiniest star,
Or monkish monotone afar,
Ye freshman's shattered accents rise,
Ye mask is lifted from his eyes.

6. To 'Varsity men this tale I speak,
For making men and killing cheek,
Stick up for your formalities,
"Ad initiandos tirones."

THE FRESHMAN'S VERSION.

N. H. Russell, '87.

1. Ye 'Varsity man has doffed his gown,
He wields a stick, but wears no frown
He sings about ye freshman's cheek,
But on him vengeance we will wreak.

2. L'Inferno's caverns are his hall,
L'Inferno's lord is at his call,
He sits upon l'Inferno's throne,
And thinks he hears ye freshman groan.

3. Ye 'Varsity men assemble 'round,
With silence awful and profound,
And judgment give in words like these—
"Ad initiandos tirones."

4. Ye minions scour earth's utmost zone,
And seize ye freshman when alone,
He's brought unto ye 'Varsity cells,
'Mid torturing jeers and miscreant yells.

5. Ye freshmen rise with one accord,
And break ye ranks of that vile horde,
They burst ye 'Varsity's flimsy chain,
And bear ye prisoner back again.

6. To freshmen all "this tale I speak,"
For quelling those who'd kill our cheek,
Down with all informalities,
"Ad conservandos tirones."

THE MAID FROM ALGOMA.

SOLO.
Adapted by J. E. J., '88.
Con animo. mf.
CHORUS.
ff
SOLO.
Voice
Piano
1. "Where are you going, my pretty maid?" Heave away, heigh - o, heigho. I'm
going to the 'Var - sity, sir," she said, "And I come away back from Al - go - ma."

CHORUS.
ff
Heave a - way! Heigh - o! Heigh - o! Heave a - way! Heigh - o! Heigh - o! "I'm
go-ing to the 'Var-si - ty, Sir," she said, "And I come a-way back from Al - go - ma."

FIRST VERSION.

1. "Where are you going, my pretty maid?"
Heave away, heigho, heigho.
"I'm going to the 'Varsity, sir," she said,
"And I come away back from Algoma."—*Cho.*

2. "What to do there, my pretty maid?"
Heave away, heigho, heigho.
"I'm going to be cultured, sir," she said,
"For I come away back from Algoma."—*Cho.*

3. "What are your studies, my pretty maid?"
Heave away, heigho, heigho.
"Chinese and Quaternions, sir," she said,
"And I come away back from Algoma."—*Cho.*

4. "Then who will marry you, my pretty maid?"
Heave away, heigho, heigho.
"Cultured girls don't marry, sir," she said,
"And I go away back to Algoma."—*Cho.*

SECOND VERSION.

1. "Where are you going, my pretty maid?"
Heave away, heigho, heigho.
"I'm going to a lecture, sir," she said,
"And I come away back from Algoma."—*Cho.*

2. "May I go with you, my pretty maid?"
Heave away, heigho, heigho.
"You wouldn't understand it, sir," she said,
"For I come away back from Algoma."—*Cho.*

3. "What is the subject, my pretty maid?"
Heave away, heigho, heigho.
"Total extinction of man," she said,
"For I go away back to Algoma."—*Cho.*

4. "Then who will marry you, my pretty maid?"
Heave away, heigho, heigho.
"— — will marry me, sir," she said,
"And I go away back to Algoma."—*Cho.*

LE BRIGADIER.

Moderato.
G. NADAUD.
VOICE.
PIANO.
1. Deux gen - dar-mes un-beau di-man - che, Chevau-chaient le long du sen-
2. Ah! c'est un mé-tier diffi - ci - le, Garan - tir la pro - pri é-
tier. L'un por - tait la sar-di-ne blan-che, L'au - tre le jau-ne baudri-
té, Dé - fen - dre les champs et la vi - le, Du vol et de l'i - ni-qui-

er. Le prem-ier , dit d'un ton so-no-re, Le temps est beau pour la sai-
té. Pour-tant l'é pou-se que j'a-do-re, Re-po-se seule à la mai-
CHORUS, (in unison).
1st and 2nd Tenor.
son. Pran, pr-r-an, pan, pan, pan, pan, pan, Pran, pr-r-an, pan, pan, pan, pan, pan, pan. Brig-a-
dier......... répondit Pan-do - - - re, Bri-ga-dier, vous avez rai-son............ Bri-ga-
1st and 2nd Bass.
Bri-ga-dier, Pan-do-re, vous a-vez rai-
dier,.......... ré-pondit Pan-do - - - - re, Bri-ga-dier, vous a-vez rai-son.
rit.
son, Brig-a-dier. Pan-do-re,

3. La gloire c'est une couronne
Faite de rose et de laurier,
J'ai servi Vénus et Bellone,
Je suis époux et brigadier;
Mais je poursuis ce météore
Qui vers Chalchos guida Jason.
Brigadier, répondit Pandore,
Brigadier, vous avez raison.

4. Phébus au bout de sa carrière
Put encore les apercevoir;
Le brigadier, de sa voix fière,
Réveillait les échos du soir:
Je vois, dit-il, le soleil qui dore
Ces verts côteaux, à l'horizon.
Brigadier, répondit Pandore,
Brigadier, vous avez raison.

5. Puis ils rêvèrent en silence;
On n'entendit plus que le pas
Des chevaux marchant en cadence,
Le brigadier ne parlait pas;
Mais quand parut la pâle aurore,
On entendit un vague son;
Brigadier, répondit Pandore, } bis.
Brigadier, vous avez raison.

OUR IRISH BEDEL.

Words by J. D. SPENCE, '89.
EMMA L. YEOMANS.
Marcato.
Voice
Piano
1. Some spake of O'Connell, the great Liberator, Of Emmett, O'Brien and Mishter Parnell; But of
2. Whin the battle was ragin' at ould Bal-a-clava, Where Irishmen nobly like Irishmen fell; In the
all E-rin's dar-lin's there's niver a cra-tur Can stand be the soide of our Irish Be-del!
thick of the fight, rushin' on like the la-va, There was no one could stop our brave Irish Bedel.
CHORUS.
Thin its
here's to his health, and his hon-or and wealth, Sure the half of his praises I niv-er could tell, Wid his
figure so straight and his il-le-gant gait, Och, there's none that can bate our brave Ir - ish Be - del.

3. Wid his sword in his hand he rode on to the battle,
And drowned all the guns wid his terrible yell;
And the Rooshans all run like a mad lot of cattle,
Wid their tails in the air, from our Irish Bedel.

4. And yez moind whin the guns on the last of October,
Woke up all the green wid their beautiful swell,
How he stood to his post all attentive and sober,
As a good soldier should, did our Irish Bedel.

5. Sure they sou't wid their gags his bould accents to stifle,
But in vain did they try his brave spirit to quell,
For he claned out the place at the end of a rifle,
Wid a bayonet fixed, did our Irish Bedel.

6. Thin its here's to his health and his honor and wealth,
Sure his virtues and graces all others excel;
He's the pride of our bosom, O ne'er may we lose him,
Nor e'er see the last of our Irish Bedel.

O TEMPORA, O MORES.

Translation by W. H. ELLIS, '67.
Allegretto.
SOLO.
CHORUS.
Voice
Piano
1. There was a jol - ly fid - dler took a walk a - long the Nile, O
crept out of the wa - - - - ter a great big cro - co - dile, O
O
O
tem - - po - ra, O mo - - - - res. There
tem - - po - ra, O mo - - - - res. He thought to make a
SOLO.
tem - - po - ra, O mo - - - - res.
tem - - po - ra, O mo - - - - res.
CHORUS.
meal of him, O was - n't that a go? O was - n't that a jol - ly lark, O
O was - n't that a go? O was - n't that a jol - ly lark, O
tem - po - ra, O - ho! .... O mu - sic charms the sav - age beast, as we all know.
tem - po - ra, O - ho! .... O mu - sic charms the sav - age beast, as we all know.

2. The fiddler drew his fiddle out, I tell you pretty quick,
O tempora, O mores;
And straight across his fiddle strings he drew his fiddle-stick,
O tempora, O mores;
Allegro, dolce, presto, now wasn't that a go?
Oh wasn't that a jolly lark, O tempora, Oho;
Oh music charms the savage beast, as we all know.

3. He had'nt played a dozen bars, before the crocodile,
O tempora, O mores;
Began to dance a Highland fling beside the ancient Nile,
O tempora, O mores;
Then polkas, galops, waltzes, oh wasn't that a go? &c.

4. Then round and round upon the sand they danced like one o'clock,
O tempora, O mores;
Until against a pyramid his tail he chanced to knock,
O tempora, O mores;
It fell and knocked six others down, oh wasn't that a go? &c.

5. Now when this awkward brute had knocked the pyramids to smash,
O tempora, O mores;
The fiddler sought the nearest pub. to try and get some hash,
O tempora, O mores;
He called for Bass's Bitter Beer, oh wasn't that a go? &c.

6. A fiddler's throat is like a hole, uncommon hard to fill,
O tempora, O mores;
And if he hasn't finished yet, no doubt he's drinking still,
O tempora, O mores;
Then let us all drink with him, O won't that be a go? &c.

THE CRUISE OF "THE BUGABOO."

Moderato
Adapted by H.H., '88 '89.
Voice
Piano
1. Come all ye ten - der heart - ed men, Wher - ev - - er ye may be, And I'll
tell - ye of the dan - - gers that are on the deep, blue sea; The

dan - gers and the hard - - ships, me byes, that I went through, When I
shipped as cook and steward, me byes, a - - boord The Bug - a - boo.
Dal Seg. for Chorus.

2. I shipped as cook and steward, me byes,
Fur divil a cint I had;
I said good-bye to Mary Ann,
And was feelin' purty bad.
As I said good-bye to Mary Ann,
And set me face to the west,
I heard the engineer remark
That the horse was doin' his best.

3. The first time that I seen the ship,
She lay in Teraulay street canal;
She was tall, an' large, an' beautiful,
Forgit her shape I niver shall.
Oh, the captain he wore a large straw hat,
Knee-breeches, and a body-coat blue;
Arrah, bedad! the byes all said, he'd make a fine figger-head
Fur to ornament *The Bugaboo*.

4. Oh, the engineer he went asleep
As he sat aboord the mule;
And the second mate called out to him
"Arrah, turn the crank, you fool!"
The second mate hollered and swore, me byes,
Till he split the back of his vest;
And the engineer woke up, and replied
That the horse was doin' his best.

5. We soon weighed anchor, an' set sail
Fur to plough the ragin' surf;
We wuz bound for the bog of Allaghen
For to git a load of turf.
We sailed all night until we reached
The back of Richmond Barracks so true;
And the gallant Eighty-Sixth fired a royal salute of bricks
At the captain of *The Bugaboo*.

6. Then the captain piped all hands on deck,
Fur to answer the salute;
And he grabbed ahold of a marlin' spike
And the second mate's left-hand boot.
He throwed the boot so straight, me byes,
That he hit the mule on the chest;
And the engineer re-mon-stra-ted
That the horse was doin' his best.

7. Nine years we sailed, when a storm arose,
The canal rose mountins high;
Oh, the lightnin' flashed, and the thunder rolled,
An' lit the dark blue sky.
The second mate he gev orders
Fur to lower the sail an' clew;
An' the captain down below, lyin' smokin' in his berth,
Set fire to *The Bugaboo*.

8. Then the mule took fright an' run away,
An' left the crew afloat;
The mate he shouted to the engineer
Fur to come and save the boat.
But the mule was gittin' along, me byes,
An' his tail was headin' for the west;
And the engineer called out quite loud
That the horse was doin' his best.

9. When the captain seen what he had done,
He loud for help did shout;
An' he hollered up troo' the chimney hole
Fur the helmsman fur to come and put it out.
But the helmsman he was fast asleep,
An' to his post untrue;
An' the fire burned so hard in the middle of the turf,
Bedad, we couldn't save *The Bugaboo*.

10. Oh, the fire it burned so hard, me byes,
That it burned the towin'-rope;
And the mule he throwed the engineer,
Who tumbled down the slope.
The captain called to the engineer
Fur to give the mule a rest;
And the engineer replied from the bank
That the horse was doin' his best.

11. When forty tousand miles from land,
In latitude fifty-four,
Oh, the fire it burned so hard, me byes,
That it couldn't burn any more;
The captain he then gev orders—
"Lower (*ad lib.*) the boats an' save the crew!"
Forty-seven Corkonians, fifty-four Far Downs,
Went down in *The Bugaboo*.

MUSH, MUSH.

Andante. mf
Voice
Piano
1. Oh, 'twas there I larned ra - din' an' wri - tin,'.......... At Billy
me we had mon - y a scrim mage,......... An'
2. Oh, 'twas there that I larned all me court - in'.......... O' the
Con - nor, she lived jist for - ninst me,.......... An'
Brac-kett's where I wint to school; And 'twas there I larned howl - in' an'
div - il a cop - y I wrote; There was ne'er a gos - soon in the
lis - sons I tuck in the art! Till Cu - pid, the blackguard, while
tin - der lines to her I wrote; If ye dare say wan hard word a-
figh - tin' Wid me school-mas-ther. Mis - ther O' Toole,.......... Him an'
vil - lage Dared.... thread on the tail o' me—
sport - in.' An ...... ar - row dhruv straight thro' me heart.......... Miss Ju - dy O'
gin her, I'll ...... thread on the tail o' yer—
1st
CHORUS.
2nd
Mush, mush, mush, tu - - ral - i ad - dy!............ Sing, mush, mush, mush,
mush, mush.

tu - ral - i - a!.......................... There was ne'er a gos - soon in the
tu - ral - i - a! If ye dare say wan hard word a-

vil - lage Dared thread on the tail o' me coat!..........
gin her, I'll thread on the tail o' yer coat!..........

3. But a blackguard, called Mickey Maloney,
Came an' sthole her affections away;
Fur he'd money an' I hadn't ony,
So I sint him a challenge nixt day.
In the ayvenin' we met at the Woodbine,
The Don we crossed o'er in a boat;
An' I lathered him wid me shillaly,
Fur he throd on the tail o' me—*Cho.*

4. Oh, me fame wint abroad through the nation,
An' folks came a-flockin' to see;
An' they cried out, widout hesitation—
"You're a fightin' man, Billy McGee!"
Oh, I've claned out the Finnigan faction,
An' I've licked all the Murphys afloat;
If you're in fur a row or a raction,
Jist ye thread on the tail o' me—*Cho.*

FORTY YEARS ON.*

Words by E. BOWEN. JOHN FARMER.

Voice.
1. For - ty years on, when a - far and a - sund-er Part-ed are those who are singing to-day,
2. Routs and dis-com - fi - tures, rush - es and ral-lies, Bas - es at-tempt-ed, and rescued and won,
Piano.
When you look back, and for - get - - ful - ly won-der What you were like in your work and your play
Strife without an - ger and art without malice,—How will it seem to you for - ty years on?

*By permission of JOHN FARMER, Esq., Balliol College, Oxford.

Then, it may be, there will of - ten come o'er you, Glimpses of notes like the catch of a song—
Then, you will say, not a fe - ver - ish minute, Strained the weak heart and the wav - er-ing knee,
p
SOLO.
Vis - ions of boyhood shall float then before you, Ec-hoes of dreamland shall bear them along. Follow
Nev - er the bat - tle raged hot - test, but in it, Neither the last nor the faintest were we!
CHORUS. SOLO. CHORUS. SOLO. CHORUS FULL CHORUS IN MARCHING TIME.
up! Follow up! Follow up! Follow up! Follow up! Follow up! Till the field ring again and a-
f
SOLO. CHORUS.
gain, With the tramp of the twenty-two men. Fol - low up! Fol - low up!

3. O the great days, in the distance enchanted,
Days of fresh air, in the rain and the sun,
How we rejoiced as we struggled and panted—
Hardly believable, forty years on!
How we discoursed of them, one with another,
Auguring triumph, or balancing fate,
Loved the ally with the heart of a brother,
Hated the foe with a playing at hate!
Follow up! &c.

4. Forty years on, growing older and older,
Shorter in wind, as in memory long,
Feeble of foot, and rheumatic of shoulder,
What will it help you that once you were strong?
God give us bases to guard or beleaguer,
Games to play out, whether earnest or fun;
Fights for the fearless, and goals for the eager,
Twenty, and thirty, and forty years on!
Follow up! &c.

KEMO KIMO.

Music adapted.
Solo. Con spirito.
Semi-Chorus.
Voice
Piano
1. A - way down south in Cen - tre street;
2. They go to bed, but it ain't no use,
Sing-song sitty, won't you ki - me - o! For their
Solo
Semi Chorus.
Dere's where de dar-keys grow ten feet;
legs hang out for a chic-ken roost.
Sing - song sit - ty won't you ki - me - o!
Full Chorus.
Ke - mo ki - mo, dar - o - wa - me - hi, me-ho - me rum - si - pum - a diddle,
soup - back piddle-winkum nim - pum, nip - cat; Sing - song sitty won't you ki - me - o!

3. Each darkey wakes up almost dead,
Sing-song sitty won't you kimeo!
With a hundredweight of chickens on each leg.
Sing-song sitty won't you kimeo!

4. The chickens go out to de barn,
Sing-song sitty won't you kimeo!
The big ones crow and the little ones larn.
Sing-song sitty won't you kimeo!

5. And when each chick is pretty full,
Sing-song sitty won't you kimeo!
He sticks his claw in the darkey's wool.
Sing-song sitty won't you kimeo!

6. I looked behind de kitchen stairs,
Sing-song sitty won't you kimeo!
I saw a caterpillar saying his prayers.
Sing-song sitty wont you kimeo,

8. (*Lento*) The horse and the sheep were going to the pasture.
Sing-song sitty won't you kimeo!
Says the horse to the sheep (*accel.*) "Won't you go a little faster?" Sing-song, &c.

THE TRAMP'S SONG.

In marching time.
Music by J. EDMUND JONES, '88.
Voice
Piano
1. 'Way down in yon - der val - ley, The mist is like a sea, Though the sun be scarcely risen, There is light enough for me. For be it car - ly morning, Or be it late at night, Cheerily ring our footsteps, Right, left, right!
2. We wan - der by the woodland, That hangs up - on the hill. Hark! the cock is tuning His morning clarion shrill. And hurried - ly a-waking From his nest a-mid the spray. Cheerily now the blackbird Whistling greets the day.
3. We gaze up - on the streamlet, As o'er the bridge we lean, We watch its hurried ripples, We watch its golden green. Oh, the men of the north are stalwart, And the woodland lasses fair, And cheerily breathes a-round us, The brac-ing woodland air.
For
CHORUS.
1ST AND 2ND TENOR.
be it car - ly morning, or be it late at night, Cheerily ring our footsteps, right, left, right. 'Mid
1ST AND 2ND BASS.

ev'ning's dusky shadows, In morning's rosy light, Cheerily ring our footsteps, Right, left, right.

O'HOOLIHAN.

Maestoso.

Voice.

Piano.

1. Me name it is O' Hoo - li - han, I'm a man of con-sid'rable in - flu-ence, I

mind my busi - ness, stay at home, Me wants be few and small; but one

rall. e dim. *a tempo*

day the byes a - round did come, All full o' whiskey, gin, and rum; And they

rall. e dim. *a tempo.*

Repeat last four bars (in unison), for Chorus.
tuk me out in the bi - lin' sun fur to play a game o' base ball.

2. They made me carry all the bats,
An' they nearly dhrove me crazy;
They put me out in the cintre-field,
But I paralyzed them all.
For I put out me fisht fur to stop a "fly,"
Whin the murtherin' thing hit me square in the eye;
An' they hung me over a fince to dhry,
The day that I played baseball.

3. I took the bat fur to strike the ball,
An' I knocked it to San Francisco,
Around the bases I did run
A dozen times or more,
Till all the byes began to howl
"O'Hoolihan ye made a foul,"
An' they rubbed me down wid a Turkish tow'l,
The day that I played baseball.

4. The editor he axed me name
Fur to give me a leather medal,
He axed me fur me fortygraft
To hang agin' the wall;
Fur he said it was me as had won the game,
Wid me head all broke, and me shoulder lame,
An' they took me home on a cattle train,
The day that I played baseball.

JINGLE, BELLS.

Allegro, mf.
Voice.
1. Dash-ing thro' the snow, In a one-horse o - pen sleigh,
2. A day or two a - go, I thought I'd take a ride, And
3. Now the ground is white; Go it while you're young,
Piano.
O'er the fields we go, Laughing all the way; Bells on bob-tail ring,
soon Miss Fannie Bright Was seated by my side. The horse was lean and lank; Mis-
Take the girls to-night, And sing this sleighing song. Just get a bob-tailed bay, Two

Making spir - its bright; What fun it is to ride and sing A sleighing song to-night!
fortune seemed his lot; He got in-to a drifted bank, And we, we got up - sot.
for - ty for his speed; Then hitch him to an open sleigh, And crack! you'll take the lead.
CHORUS.
TENORS.
Jingle, bells! jingle, bells! jingle all the way........................
jin-gle, jin-gle, jin-gle,
BASSES.
Jingle, jingle, jingle, jingle, all the way...
PIANO.
Oh! what fun it is to ride In a one-horse open sleigh......... Jingle, bells, jingle, bells,
one-horse open sleigh. Jingle, jingle, jingle, jingle,

jingle all the way,..............Oh! what fun it is to ride In a one-horse open sleigh!
jingle, jingle, jingle,
jingle all the way,..............Oh! what fun it is to ride In a one-horse open sleigh!

THE FRESHMAN'S FATE;

OR, THE PERILS OF CO-EDUCATION.

Tune—"JINGLE, BELLS."

J. D. SPENCE, '89.

1. Come youths and maidens all,
   Just listen while I tell,
Of a 'Varsity undergrad,
   And what to him befel.
He was a merry lad,
   And laughing all the day,
For thus it was he strove
To drive dull care away.

CHORUS.

Ha! Ha! Ha! Ha! Ha! Ha!
   Laughing all the day
Oh! what fun it is to laugh,
   And drive dull care away. (*Bis*)

2. But one bright day there came
   A maiden to the college:
Her face was full of charms,
   Her head was full of knowledge,
He looked and looked again
   Upon the lovely sight;
He watched her all the day,
   And dreamt of her all night.
      Chorus.—Ha! Ha! Ha! &c.

3. And so it came to pass
   She stole his heart away;
He grew quite thin and pale,
   And pined the livelong day
He worse and worse did grow,
   Until—most awful doom,
The skeleton he became
   In the Biology room.

CHORUS.

Ha! Ha! Ha! Ha! Ha! Ha!
   Laughing all the day,
Oh! what fun it is to laugh,
   And drive dull care away. (*Bis.*)

4. And should you chance to tread
   At midnight's solemn hour,
Along the passage dread
   Of the western corridor,
You'll hear a gruesome sound,
   Your hair will stand with fear,
'Tis the skeleton's voice profound,
   In accents hoarse and drear.
      Chorus.—Ha! Ha! Ha! &c.

THERE IS A TAVERN IN THE TOWN.

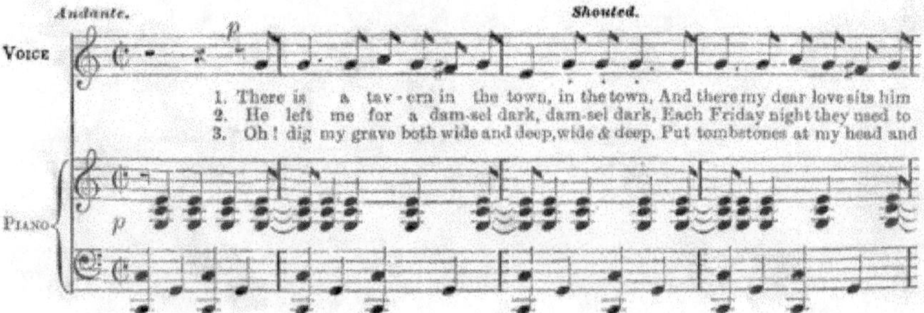
Andante.
Shouted.
VOICE
1. There is a tav - ern in the town, in the town, And there my dear love sits him
2. He left me for a dam-sel dark, dam-sel dark, Each Friday night they used to
3. Oh! dig my grave both wide and deep, wide & deep, Put tombstones at my head and
PIANO
p

down, sits him down, And drinks his wine 'mid laugh - ter free, And nev - er, never thinks of
spark, used to spark, And now my love, once true to me, Takes that dark damsel on his
feet, head and feet, And on my breast carve a tur - tle dove, To sig - ni - fy I died of
CHORUS.
me.
knee. Fare thee well, for I must leave thee, Do not let the parting grieve thee, And re-
love.
member that the best of friends must part, must part. A-dieu, adieu, kind friends, adieu, adieu, adieu, I
can no long - er stay with you, stay with you. I'll hang my harp on a

1st & 2nd.
weeping willow tree, And may the world go well with thee.
well with thee, thee, well with thee.

SEEING NELLIE HOME.

Andante.

Voice

Piano

p

1. In the sky the bright stars glittered,....... On the bank the pale moon shone; And 'twas from Aunt Dinah's quilting party I was see - ing Nellie home...
2. On my arm a soft hand rested,........ Rest-ed light as o cean foam; And 'twas from Aunt Dinah's quilting party I was see - ing Nellie home.......

CHORUS.

p *cresc.* *f*

I was see - ing Nel - lie home,........I was see - ing Nel - lie home; And 'twas

ff *repeat pp*

from Aunt Di - nah's quilt-ing par - ty I was see - - ing Nel - lie home.

3. On my lips a whisper trembled,
Trembled till it dared to come;
And 'twas from Aunt Dinah's quilting party,
I was seeing Nellie home.

4. On my life new hopes were dawning,
And those hopes have lived and grown;
And 'twas from Aunt Dinah's quilting party,
I was seeing Nellie home.

POLLY-WOLLY-DOODLE.

Allegro. SOLO. CHORUS.
VOICE.
PIANO.
1. Oh, I went down South for to see my Sal; Sing "Pol-ly-wol-ly-doo-dle" all the
2. Oh, my Sal she am a...... maid-en fair: Sing "Pol-ly-wol-ly-doo-dle" all the
SOLO. CHORUS.
day! My Sal-ly am a spunk-y gal, Sing "Polly-wolly-doodle" all the
day! With laugh-ing eyes and cur-ly hair, Sing "Polly-wolly-doodle" all the
CHORUS.
day! Fare-well!......... Fare-well!........ Fare-well, my fai-ry fay! Oh, I'm
day! Bass. Fare thee well! Fare thee well! Fare thee well! Fare thee well!
off to Louisi-an-a, for to see my Su-sy An-na, Singing "Polly-wolly-doodle" all the day!

3. Oh! I came to a river, an' I couldn't get across,
Sing "Polly-wolly-doodle," all the day.
An' I jumped upon a nigger, for I thought he was a hoss,
Sing "Polly-wolly-doodle," all the day.

4. Oh! a grasshopper sittin' on a railroad track,
Sing "Polly-wolly-doodle," all the day.
A-pickin' his teef wid a carpet tack,
Sing "Polly-wolly-doodle," all the day.

5. Behind de barn, down on my knees,
Sing "Polly-wolly-doodle," all the day.
I thought I heard a chicken sneeze,
Sing "Polly-wolly-doodle," all the day.

6. He sneezed so hard wid de hoopin'-cough,
Sing "Polly-wolly-doodle," all the day.
He sneezed his head an' his tail right off,
Sing "Polly-wolly-doodle," all the day

SAILING, SAILING, SAILING.

Dolce. Tempo di valse. mf
Words by W. J. HEALY, '88.
VOICE.
PIANO.
1. Ov - er the riv - - er, ov - er the Dee, Dwells.... a maid - en fair............... Oh! laugh - - ing lips and eyes...... has she, and ripp - - ling, sun - - ny hair...............
2. Up to her win - - dow, sun - shine or rain, A clamb' - ring rose - - vine goes............... And over the river my heart would fain To climb with the climb - - ing rose..............
YODEL. La la yo - - del la yo - - del la yo - del la la la la yo - del la yo - del la la la la la la yo - del la
Sail - - ing, sail - - ing, Sail - - ing, Sail - - ing down the stream.......... Sail - - ing
Vocal or instrumental accompaniment.
la la la la
zum zum

yo - del la yo - del la la la la la la la la la la la la.
Sail - - ing, sail - - - - ing, Sail - - ing down . . . . the stream.
la la la la la la la la la la la la la la la
zum zum zum zum zum zum

3. After the sunset flush has flown,
   When lilacs scent the air,
   By the old bridge I'll meet alone
   My love so blithe and fair.

4. Over the river, the evening breeze
   Fragrance-laden blows;
   Under the blossoming apple trees,
   I walk with my lovely Rose.

5. Eyes has my love like a day in June,
   When all the sky is blue,—
   Lips like a rose in a summer noon,
   Ripe-red through and through.

6. Ever I dream of one sweetest word
   I to my love will say;
   Oh, my heart is like a singing-bird
   On a swaying hazel spray.

H_2SO_4.

1. DIRECTIONS. You take a few pieces of zinc, And put in your gen - er - a - tor, Add
2. OBSERVATIONS. The ac - tion was not ver - y brisk, When I put in H 2 S O 4, So I
3. CONCLUSIONS. As I wiped up the a-cid and zinc, And swept up the glass from the floor, I con-
wa - ter, then plug in the cork, and pour in H 2 S O 4. And
tried ni - tric a - cid to see If the thing would'nt bub - ble up more, If the
clud - ed I'd stick to directions, And try my own me - thods no more, And
CHORUS.
pour in H 2 S O 4. And pour in H 2 S O 4. Add
thing would'nt bub - ble up more, If the thing wouldn't bub - ble up more, So I
try my own me - thods no more, And try my own me - thods no more, I con-
wa - ter then plug in the cork, And pour in H 2 S O 4
tried ni - tric a - cid to see If the thing wouldn't bub - ble up more.
clud - ed I'd stick to di - rec - tions, And try my own meth - ods no more.

ROW YOUR BOAT.

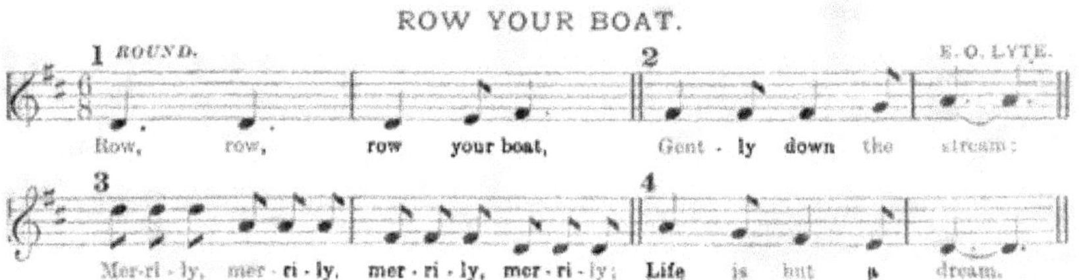
1 ROUND.
E. O. LYTE.
2
Row, row, row your boat, Gent - ly down the stream;
3
4
Mer-ri - ly, mer - ri - ly, mer - ri - ly, mer - ri - ly; Life is but a dream.

OH MY DARLING CLEMENTINE.

Tempo di mazurka.
Words and Music by PERCY MONTROSE.
Voice
Piano
1. In a cab-in, in a can-on, an ex-ca-va-tion for a mine; Dwelt a min-er, A For-ty-nin-er, And his daugh-ter Cle-men-tine.
2. She drove her duck-lets To the riv-er, Ev'ry morning just at nine; Stubbed her toe a-gainst a sliv-er, Fell in-to the foaming brine.
3. Ru-by lips A-bove the wa-ter, Blowing bubbles soft and fine; Alas for me, I was no swimmer, So I lost my Clemen-tine.
CHORUS.
Air.
1st Tenor.
Basses.
Oh my dar-ling Oh my dar-ling, Oh my dar-ling Cle-men-tine,........You are lost and gone for-ev-er, Dref-ful sor-ry, Cle-men-tine.
Cle-men-tine. Cle-men-tine, Cle-men-Cle-men-tine, Cle-men-Clemen-tine, Cle-men-tine, Clementine, Clemen-Cle-men-tine.
Oh Cle-men-tine, Oh Cle-men-tine, Oh Cle-men-Cle-men-tine, Cle-men-Clemen-tine, Cle-men-tine, Oh Clementine, Oh Clemen-Cle-men-tine.

MY BONNIE.

Andante. Dolce.
Voice.
Piano.
1. My Bonnie is over the ocean, My Bonnie is over the sea.............. My Bonnie is over the ocean, Oh bring back my Bonnie to me..............
2. Oh, blow ye winds over the ocean, Oh blow ye winds over the sea.............. Oh blow ye winds over the ocean, And bring back my Bonnie to me..............
8va
CHORUS.
Air
p
cres.
Bring back, bring back, bring back my Bonnie to me, to me.
Tenor and 1st Bass.
Bring back, bring back, bring back my Bonnie to me, to me.
2nd Bass.

D. C.
Bring back, bring back, O bring back my Bon - nie to me.
Bring back, bring back, O bring back my Bon nie to me.........

3. Last night as I lay on my pillow,
Last night as I lay on my bed,
Last night as I lay on my pillow,
I dreamed that my Bonnie was dead.
Chorus—Bring back, etc.

4. The winds have blown over the ocean,
The winds have blown over the sea,
The winds have blown over the ocean,
And brought back my Bonnie to me.
Chorus—Bring back, etc.

UBI BENE, IBI PATRIA.

Moderato. *mf.*
1. All the world a - round I'm stray-ing, Eve - ry sea and mountain o'er;
2. All my goods weigh not a fea - ther, And my blood is nev - er old;
3. In my heart are all my treas-ures— Joys no hand can take a way;
Lively. *ff*
Free as air, I'm nev - er staying On the North or Southern shore, Mer-ry here and mer-ry there,
Eve-ry-where I feast with princes, Eve-ry-where in halls of gold. Hungry here and hungry there,
Who would pine for Mammon's pleasures Death can darken in a day. Mer-ry here and mer-ry there,
rall.
U - bi Be - ne, i - bi Pa - tri - a, U - bi Be - ne, i - bi, Pa - tri - a.

4. While my pipe is yet beside me,
And my beer remains to foam,
With a hat and coat to hide me,
Everywhere I'll gaily roam.
Drinking here and smoking there (*Bis.*)
Ubi Bene, ibi Patria (*Bis*).

5. In the bowl I'm ever heeding
Love's delicious, maddening glow;
Now in northland humbly pleading,
Now were southern breezes blow.
Kissing here and drinking there (*Bis.*)
Ubi Bene, ibi Patria (*Bis.*)

6. So through life I'm smoothly gliding
On a calm and shining sea,
Sorrow's clouds in kisses hiding,
And in wine's sweet revelry.
Merry here and merry there (*Bis.*)
Ubi Bene, ibi Patria (*Bis.*)

7. By-and-by shall Death's grim shadows
On this useless clay be laid;
Then I'll clasp the cooling meadows
In the golden land of shade!
Merry here and merry there (*Bis.*)
Ubi Bene, ibi Patria (*Bis.*)

ALMA MATER.

CHORUS.
1st & 2nd TENORS
AIR
2ND BASS
Oh, Al - ma Ma - - ter! Thus I think, and then I sigh.
Hard is thy fet - - ter, When a pret - ty girl is nigh.
FINE.
SOLO.
I'm heart - 'ly tired of Greece and Rome, I wear - y through each learn - ed tome. I
won - der how can pleas - ure come In thinking of x plus y..........
D.C.

1. I'm heartily tired of Greece and Rome,
   I weary through each learned tome.
   I wonder how can pleasure come
   In thinking of x plus y.
   Chorus.—Oh Alma Mater! &c.

2. When morning comes, oh then, oh then,
   Whether at eight, or nine, or ten,
   Up I must get from my cosy den,
   And off to college fly.
   Chorus.—Oh Alma Mater! &c

3. And then, oh then, on a winter's night,
   With one on my left and one on my right,
   'Tis pleasant thus to walk at night,
   Don't ask me the reason why.
   Chorus.—Oh Alma Mater! &c.

4. Summer is coming, and naught like this,
   Lolling all day on banks of bliss,
   And now and then a-stealing a kiss,
   And if I can't I'll try.
   Chorus.—Oh Alma Mater! &c.

THE SPANISH GUITAR.

Moderato. mf.
Adapted by W. J. H. and J. E. J.
Voice.
1. When I was a stu - dent at Ca - diz,.......... I
Piano.
mf.
played on the Span - ish gui - tar, ching, ching! I used to make love to the
la - dies,.......... I think of them still from a - far, ching, ching!
CHORUS.
Tra la la la, tra la la la, tra la la la, tra la la la, tra la la la.
Ring, ching, ching! Ring, ching, ching! Ring out ye bells, Oh ring out ye

Tra la la la, tra la la la, tra la la la, tra la la la, tra la la la
bells, Oh ring out ye bells! Ring ching ching! Ring ching ching!
Tra la la la, tra la la la, tra la la la, tra la la la, tra la la la,

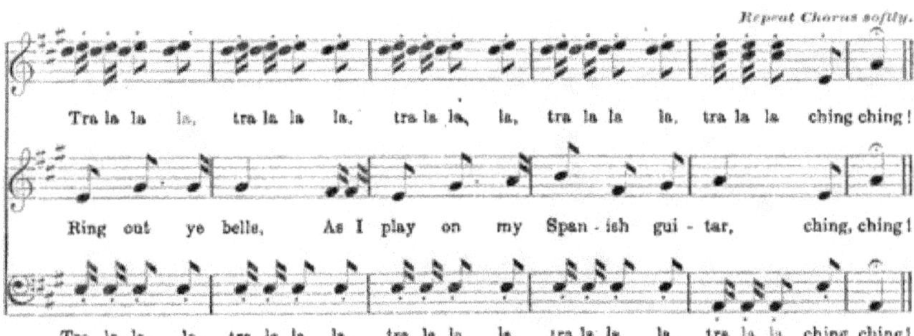
Repeat Chorus softly.
Tra la la la, tra la la la, tra la la, la, tra la la la, tra la la ching ching!
Ring out ye bells, As I play on my Span - ish gui - tar, ching, ching!
Tra la la la, tra la la la, tra la la la, tra la la la, tra la la ching, ching!

2. I was four years a student at Cadiz,
   Where nothing one's pleasure can mar, ching, ching!
 And where many a beautiful maid is,—
   Oh I strumm'd and I twang'd my guitar, ching, ching!

3. Oh I sang serenades there at Cadiz,
   Till I got an attack of catarrh, ching, ching!
 Though no more I could serenadize,
   Still I played on my Spanish guitar, ching, ching!

4. When at last the train bore me from Cadiz,
   The ladies all wept round the car, ching, ching!
 Oh it grieved to me to part from those ladies,
   But I carried away my guitar, ching, ching!

5. I'm no longer a student at Cadiz,
   But I play on the Spanish guitar, ching, ching!
 And still I am fond of the ladies,
   Though now I'm a happy papa, ching, ching!

A TALE OF TWO IDLES.

TUNE—"THE SPANISH GUITAR."

Words by MADGE R. ROBERTSON, '89.

1. Now we'll sing you a song of two idles,
   Who idled by night and by day; ding dong;
 Who idled round "Varsity" precincts
   One year from October to May; ding dong.

CHORUS (very slowly).

Ding dong ding, ding dong ding, toll out ye bells!
   Oh, toll out ye bells! oh, toll out ye bells!
Ding dong ding, ding dong ding, toll out ye bells!
   As we chant this most doleful refrain; ding dong.

2. They "posed" idly about at the doorway,
   Waiting letters—nay, duns, we should say; ding dong;
 And ogled the girls, who, in passing,
   Could see but a tattered array; ding dong.
   Chorus—Ding dong ding, etc.

3. Sometimes they strolled into a lecture
   To idle an hour away; ding dong;
 Next, dinner took up all attention,
   Then football the rest of the day; ding dong.
   Chorus—Ding dong ding, etc.

4. They idled through divers flirtations,
   And idled at last into love; ding dong;
 But alas for the charms of our idles,
   Their idols most faithless did prove; ding, dong.
   Chorus—Ding dong ding, etc.

5. Then last, idly fell in a "fixed system,"
   A piece of red ribbon and blue; ding dong;
 Went up on a "complex idea,"
   And to life bid a last fond adieu; ding dong.
   Chorus—Ding dong ding, etc.

PETER GRAY.

Andante.
VOICE.
1. Once on a time there was a man, his name was Pe - ter Gray;
PIANO.
p
cres.
He lived way down in that 'ere town, called Pen - syl - va - ni - a.
CHORUS.
Blow ye winds of the morn - - ing, Blow ye winds, Heigh - o,......
p
pp
p
Blow ye winds of the morn - - ing, Blow, blow, blow.

2. Now Peter Gray he fell in love, all with a nice young girl,
The first three letters of her name were L-U-C, Anna Quirl.—*Cho.*

3. But just as they were going to wed, her papa he said "No!"
And consequently she was sent away off to Ohio.—*Cho.*

4. And Peter Gray he went to trade for furs and other skins,
Till he was caught and scalp - y - ed by the bloody Indians.—*Cho.*

5. When Lucy Anna heard the news, she straightway took to bed,
And never did get up again until she di - i - ed.—*Cho.*

DEAR EVELINA, SWEET EVELINA.

Allegretto, mf
Voice.
1. Way down in the mead-ow where the li - ly first blows, Where the
fond Ev - e - li - na, the sweet lit - tle dove, The
2. She's fair as a rose, like a lamb she is meek, And she
most grace - ful curls hangs her ra - ven black hair, And
Piano
1st
2nd
wind from the mountains ne'er ruf - fles the rose; Lives
pride of the val - ley, the .... girl that I love.
nev - er was known to put paint on her cheek; In the
she nev - er re - quires .... per - fum - ery there.
CHORUS.
f
Dear Ev - e - lin - a, sweet Ev - e - lin - a,
(1st Tenor.)
Air.
my dar - ling boy,.......... For
he was
thee shall nev - - er, nev - er die.
Repeat Chorus pp
nd his name was Mich - ael Roy!...

sweet Ev - e - lin - a, My love for thee shall nev - er, nev-er die.

3. Evelina and I, one fine evening in June,
Took a walk all alone by the light of the moon,
The planets all shone, for the heavens were clear,
And I felt round the heart most tremendously queer.—*Cho.*

4. Three years have gone by, and I've not got a dollar,
Evelina still lives in that green grassy holler,
Although I am fated to marry her never,
I've sworn that I'll love her for ever and ever.—*Cho.*

MICHAEL ROY.

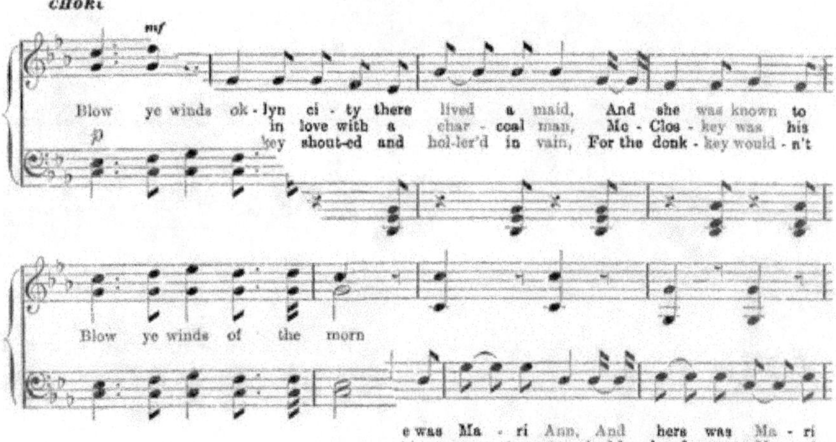
CHORt
mf
Blow ye winds ok - lyn ci - ty there lived a maid, And she was known to
in love with a char - coal man, Mc - Clos - key was his
p
key shout-ed and hol-ler'd in vain, For the donk - key would - n't
Blow ye winds of the morn
e was Ma - ri Ann, And hers was Ma - ri
at was seven stone ten, And he loved sweet Ma - ri
right ov - er his head, Right in - to a pol - i - cy

2. Now Peter Gray he fell in lov
The first three letters of her n

3. But just as they were going to
And consequently she was sen

4. And Peter Gray he went to tr
Till he was caught and scalp -

5. When Lucy Anna heard the
And never did get up again u

Jane;........ And ev-ery Sat-ur-day morn- - ing She used to go ov-er the
Jane;........ He took her to ride in his char-coal cart On a fine Saint Pat-rick's
shop;........ When Mc-Clos-key saw that ter - ri-ble sight, His heart it was moved with
riv-er, And went to market where she sold eggs, And sass-a-ges, like-wise liv-er......
day, But the donkey took fright at a Jer - sey man, And start-ed and ran a - - way.....
pi - ty, So he stabbed the donkey with a bit of charcoal, And started for Salt Lake ci - ty.......
CHORUS.
For oh!.......... For oh!..........
(1st Tenor.)
For oh! For oh! he was my dar - ling boy,.......... For
Air.
For oh! For oh! he was
ff
For oh! For oh!
Repeat Chorus pp
he was the lad with the au - burn hair, And his name was Mich - ael Roy!......

AMO, AMAS, I LOVE A LASS.

Tune—"The Mouse and the Frog." DR. ARNOLD.

Voice.
Piano
1. A - mo, A - mas, I love a lass, As a ce - dar
2. Oh, how bel - - la my pu - - el - - la, I'll kiss se - cu
tall and slend - - er. Sweet cow - slip's grace is her nom-in - ative
la se - cu - lo - - rum. If I've luck, sir, she's my
case, And she's of the fe - mi - nine gen - - - - der.
ux - - or, O di - - es be - ne - dic - - to - - - - rum!
CHORUS.
Ro - rum, Co - rum, sunt di - - vo - rum, Ha - rum, sca - rum, di - - vo;
Tag rag, merry derry, per - i - wig and hat - band Hic hoc ho - rum ge - ni

ti . . . . vo!
mf
8va.

ALOUETTE.

Moderato. mf — French-Canadian.

Voice. Piano.

1. A - lou - et - te, gen-tille A - lou - et - te, A - lou - et - te, je te plu - me - rai,
Je te plu - me - rai la tête, je te plu - me - rai la tête, * et la tête, O..........

CHORUS. 2nd Tenors. 1st Ten. 1st Bass. 2nd Bass. *f*
et la tête, O..

f A - lou - et - te, gen-tille A - lou - et - te, A - lou - et - te, je te plu - me - rai.

2. Alouette, gentille Alouette, Alouette, je te plumerai,
Je te plumerai le bec, je te plumerai le bec,
Et le bec, et le bec, et la tête, et la tête.—O, &c.

3. Alouette, gentille Alouette, Alouette, je te plumerai,
Je te plumerai le nez, je te plumerai le nez,
Et le nez, et le nez, et le bec, et le bec,
Et la tête, et la tête.—O, &c.

4. Alouette, gentille Alouette, Alouette, je te plumerai,
Je te plumerai le dos, je te plumerai le dos,
Et le dos, et le dos, et le nez, et le nez,
Et le bec, et le bec, et la tête, et la tête.—O, &c.

5. Alouette, gentille Alouette, Alouette, je te plumerai,
Je te plumerai les pattes, je te plumerai les pattes,
Et les pattes, et les pattes, et le dos, et le dos,
Et le nez, et le nez, et le bec, et le bec,
Et la tête, et la tête.—O, &c.

6. Alouette, gentille Alouette, Alouette, je te plumerai,
Je te plumerai le cou, je te plumerai le cou,
Et le cou, et le cou, et les pattes, et les pattes,
Et le dos, et le dos, et le nez, et le nez,
Et le bec, et le bec, et la tête, et la tête.—O, &c.

* Repeat this bar once for 2nd verse, twice for 3rd, etc.

A-ROVING.

Allegretto. mf SOLO
CHORUS
SOLO
VOICE.
PIANO
At number three Old England Square, Mark well what I do say; At
number three Old England Square, My Nancy Dawson she lived there: And I'll go no more a-
rov - - ing With you, fair maid!
CHORUS
A - - rov ing! A - - rov - ing! Since
f
rov - ing's been my ru - i - in, I'll go no more a rov - - ing With you, fair maid!

2. My Nancy Dawson she lived there,
Mark well what I do say;
She was a lass surpassing fair,
She'd bright blue eyes and golden hair;
And I'll go no more a-roving
With you, fair maid.
Chorus.—A-roving, &c.

3. I met her first when home from sea,
Mark well what I do say;
Home from the coast of Africkee,
With pockets lined with good monie;
And I'll go no more a-roving
With you, fair maid.
Chorus.—A-roving, &c.

4. Oh! didn't I tell her stories true,
Mark well what I do say;
And didn't I tell her whoppers too!
Of the gold we found in Timbuctoo;
And I'll go no more a-roving
With you, fair maid.
Chorus.—A-roving, &c.

5. But when we'd spent my blooming "screw,"
Mark well what I do say;
And the whole of the gold from Timbuctoo,
She cut her stick and vanished too;
And I'll go no more a-roving
With you, fair maid.
Chorus—A-roving, &c.

THE UNDERGRADUATE'S LAMENT.

Air—"To All You Ladies now on Land."
Words by PRESIDENT WILSON.
Allegro con animo.
Tenors
Bass.
To Chan-cel - lor and Sen - ate too, We men in Hall in - dite; We
wish that you could real-ly know How hard it is to write; When facts are scarce, i-
de - - as few, the pa - pers are such po - sers too, such po - - sers too.
2nd time Chorus.
with a fal................
With a fal lal la la la la la, With a fal lal la la la la la, With a
fal lal la la la, with a fal lal la la la with a fal lal la la la la la.
fal lal la, with a fal lal la with a fal lal la la la.
FINE.

2. Make some of those examiners
   Just try their hands for once,
 And let us be the questioners,
   And see who is the dunce!
 The papers that they think so wise
 I guess would take them by surprise.
   With a fal, lal, la, etc.

3. Compare coördinates by steps
   Cartesian, and tell
 Why an eclipse and an ellipse
   Just differ by an ell.
 Next solve equation $a + b$
 By — of the Q.E.D.
   With a fal, lal, la, etc.

4. Define the mean apparent time
   Examinations last;
 And how ideas come so slow
   When minutes fly so fast?
 Perdidi diem, anyway
 Time's up, and I have lost the day.
   With a fal, lal, la, etc.

5. Look here, McKim, this pen's a rig,
   Will neither write nor spell.
 Did Julius Cæsar wear a wig?
   Can anybody tell?
 I give it up. Confound the fool!
 Send back th' examiner to school!
   With a fal, lal, la, etc.

THE PIPE.

Tune—A Wet Sheet and A Flowing Sea.

Voice.
Piano.
Of all things on earth that to joy give birth, And rend - er a man's heart
jol - ly, There's not I'm sure a bet - ter cure Than a pipe for mel - an-
choi - y. It can make a tiff pass off with a whiff, And the joys of content - ment
borrow, And the worst wars cease in a pipe of peace, Which soothes the nerves of sor-row.
CHORUS.
Then hur - rah for the pipe so rich and ripe, with its am - ber mouth so

yel - low. And the curl-ing smoke that doth e - voke A fragrance mild and mellow.

2 Let philosophers rant of Fichte and Kant,
Of Hartley and his vibrations,
And puzzle their wits with Clarke, Leibnitz,
Time, space, and their relations;
Yet six feet space will end their race,
And prove their sciences trashes,
While Time with a wipe will break their pipe,
And Death knock out the ashes.
Chorus.—Then hurrah, &c.

3. Let the soldier boast of the mighty host,
Of the pride and the pomp of battle,
Of the war steed's bound, and the clarion's sound,
And the cannon's thundering rattle;
Yet there's more delight with a friend at night,
And a song and a pipe also,
Than in balls and bombs, and fifes and drums,
And military show.
Chorus.—Then hurrah, &c.

THE BOOTS.

Moderato. *mf*

Voice.

Piano.

1. The fes - tal day has come, And bright - ly beams the morn - ing; The sun peeps forth a-fresh, Our fest - al day a-dorn - ing. Hurrah! Hurrah! The
2. Come, join in mirth and song, With young hearts fond - ly beat - ing, Sip plea-sure while we may, For earth-ly joys are fleet-ing.

CHORUS. In unison.

fest - al day has come! Hur-rah! Hur-rah! The fest - al day has come.

Allegro vivace. f
*Up - see, upsee, tra la la la, Up-see, up - see, tra la la la, Up - see, up-see, tra la la la, The
p
fes - tal day has come, I hear the boots, the boots, the boots the b - b - b - b - b - b - boots, Fra Di-
ff
a - vo-lo, the Rob-ber! Fra Di - a - vo - lo, the Rob - ber! I hear the boots, the boots, the boots, the
p
b - b - b - b - b - b - boots, Fra Di - a - vo - lo the Rob - ber, Coming down the stairs.
ff
sec.

THERE'S ONLY ROOM FOR ONE.

Tenors
Spoken by one.
Why have the faculty but one idea?
Shouted by all
BECAUSE!
There's on - ly room for one, There's on - ly room for one; At the
Bass
Piano
Residence gate at half-past eight, Keeping the porter up so late, There's only room for one.... There's
on - ly room for one; At the Residence gate at half-past eight, There's only room for one.

2. Why is there but one *real* University in America?

3 Why didn't "Queen's" come into Confederation?

4. Why has the Chicago girl but one foot in the grave?

Local hits should be introduced.

INTEGER VITÆ.

HOR., Lib. I, C. XXII. FLEMMING, 1778-1813.

Andante.
Tenors
Basses
1. In - te - ger vi - tæ sce - le - ris - que pu - rus Non e - get
2. Siv - e per Syr - tes i - ter æs - tu - o - sas Siv - e fac
3. Nam - que me sil - va lu - pus in Sa - bi - na Dum me-am
Mau - - - ris jac - u - lis nec ar - - - cu, Nec ve - ne - - - na - - - tis
tu - - - rus per in - hos - pi - ta - - lem Cau - - ca - sum vel quæ
can - - to Lal - a - gen, et ul - - - tra Ter - mi - num cu - - - ris
gra - vi - da sa - git - - tis, Fus - ce, pha - - re - - - - tra.
lo - ca fab - u - - lo - - sus Lam - bit Hy - - das - - - - pes,
va - gor ex - pe - - di - - tis Fu - git in - - er - - - mem.
4. Quale portentum neque militaris
Daunias latis alit æsculetis;
Nec Jubæ tellus generat, leonum
Arida nutrix.
5. Pone me, pigris ubi nulla campis
Arbor æstiva recreatur aura;
Quod latus mundi nebulæ malusque
Jupiter urget.
6. Pone sub curru nimium propinqui
Solis, in terra domibus negata;
Dulce ridentem Lalagen amabo,
Dulce loquentem.
MEERSCHAUM PIPE.
Expressivo.
Arranged by THEO. MARTENS.
Tenors.
1. Oh, who will smoke my meerschaum pipe,
Air.
Oh, who will smoke my meerschaum pipe, Oh,
2nd Bass.
Oh, who will smoke my meerschaum pipe, Meerschaum pipe,
Piano.

Oh, who will smoke my
Oh who will smoke my meerschaum pipe,
Oh who will smoke my
who will smoke my meerschaum pipe,
Oh, who
will smoke my
Oh, who will smoke my meerschaum pipe, Meerschaum pipe
Oh, who will

meerschaum pipe when I, when I am far a - way
meerschaum pipe when I am far, When I am far a - way.
† Bad man!
meerschaum pipe When I am far a - way.
Bad man!
smoke my meerschaum pipe When I am far a-way.
*Allie Bazan!
Bad man!

2. Oh, who will wear my cast-off boots?
Allie Bazan! Johnnie Moran!

3. Oh, who will hoist my green umbrell?
Allie Bazan, Johnnie Moran, Mary McCann!

4. Oh, who will go to see my girl?
Allie Bazan, Johnnie Moran, Mary McCann,
Kazecazan!

5. Oh, who will take her out to ride?
Allie Bazan, Johnnie Moran, Mary McCann,
Kazecazan, Yucatan!

6. Oh, who will squeeze her snow-white hand?
Allie Bazan, Johnnie Moran, Mary McCann,
Kazecazan, Yucatan, Kalamazoo!

7. Oh, who will trot her on his knee?
Allie Bazan, Johnnie Moran, Mary McCann,
Kazecazan, Yucatan, Kalamazoo, Michigan!

8. Oh, who will kiss ner ruby lips?
Allie Bazan, Johnnie Moran, Mary McCann,
Kazecazan, Yucatan, Kalamazoo, Michigan,
BAD MAN!!!

* Repeat this strain once for second stanza, twice for third, etc.

† For last stanza only.

SON OF A GAMBOLIER.

Con moto.
Voice.
Piano.
1. I'm a rambling rake of pov - er - ty, From Tippe'ry town I came; 'Twas
2. I once was tall and hand - some, And was so ver - y neat, They
3. I'm a rambling wretch of pov - er - ty, From Tippe'ry town I came; My
pov er - ty compelled me first to go out in the rain., In all sorts of weather, Be it
thought I was too good to live, Most good enough to eat. But now I'm old, My coat is torn, And
coat I bought from an old Jew shop Way down in Maiden Lane; My hat I got from a sailor lad Just
wet or be it dry, I am bound to get my live-li-hood, Or lay me down and die.
pover-ty holds me fast, And ev - ry girl turns up her nose As I go wand'ring past.
eighteen years gone by, And my shoes I picked from an old dust-heap, Which ev'ry one shunned but I.
CHORUS.
Air.
Come join my hum-ble dit-ty, From Tippe'ry Town I steer, Like eve - ry hon - est fel-low, I
1st Tenor.
Come join my hum-ble dit-ty, From Tippe'ry Town I steer, Like eve - ry hon - est fel-low, I
1st Bass.
2nd Bass.

drinks my la - ger beer ; Like eve - ry jol - ly fellow, I takes my whiskey clear. I'm a
drinks my la - ger beer ; Like eve - ry jol - ly fellow, I takes my whiskey clear. I'm a
rambling rake of pov - er-ty, And the son of a Gambolier, The son of a son of a son of a son of a
rambling rake of pov - er-ty, And the son of a Gambolier, The son of a son of a son of a son of a
son of a Gam - bolier, The son of a son of a son of a son of a son of a Gam - bolier. Like
son of a Gam - bolier, The son of a son of a son of a son of a son of a Gam - bolier. Like
ev'ry jol-ly fellow I takes my whiskey clear, I'm a rambling rake of poverty, And the son of a Gambolier.
ev'ry jol-ly fellow I takes my whiskey clear, I'm a rambling rake of poverty, And the son of a Gambolier.

THE LANDLADY'S DAUGHTER.

Translation by J. EDMUND JONES, '88.

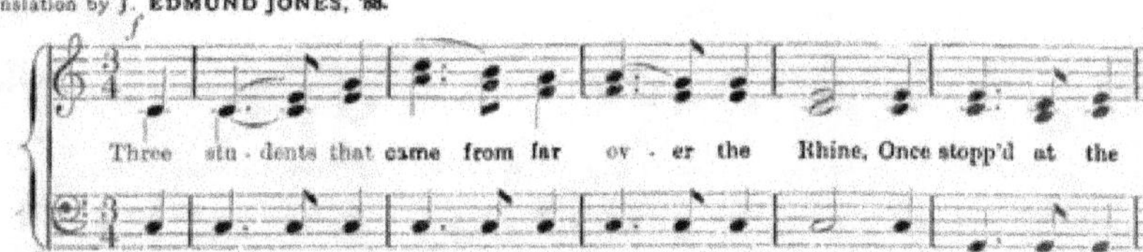
Three stu - dents that came from far ov - er the Rhine, Once stopp'd at the

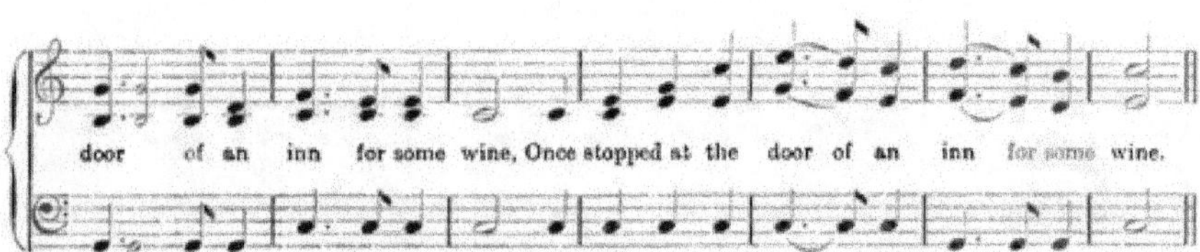
door of an inn for some wine, Once stopped at the door of an inn for some wine.

1. Three students that came from far over the Rhine,
   Once stopped at the door of an inn for some wine.
2. "Kind landlady, have you good wine I pray?
   And where is your charming young daughter to-day?"
3. "My beer and my wine are refreshing and clear.
   In her heavenly home is my daughter so dear."
4. And when they stopped into the chamber of death,
   They gazed on the maiden and each held his breath.
5. The veil from her face the first drew aside,
   And looked at her sadly, and mournfully cried:
6. "Ah! didst thou but live, oh maiden so pure!
   From this very moment I'd love thee, I'm sure.
7. The veil o'er her face the second one drew,
   And wept as he turned from the sorrowful view.
8. "Alas, that thou thus liest dead on thy bier!
   For thee I have loved since many a year."
9. The third moved again the veil from its place,
   And bent o'er the form, and kissed the pale face
10. "Thee always I loved, thee love I to-day,
    And thee shall I love for ever and aye."

DER WIRTHIN TÖCHTERLEIN.

UHLAND, 1813.

1. *Es zogen drei Bursche wohl über den Rhein,*
   Bei einer Frau Wirthin, da kehrten sie ein.
2. *„Frau Wirthin, hat sie gut Bier und Wein?*
   Wo hat sie ihr schönes Töchterlein?"
3. *„Mein Bier und Wein ist frisch und klar,*
   Mein Töchterlein liegt auf der Todtenbahr."
4. *Und als sie traten zur Kammer hinein,*
   Da lag sie in einem schwarzen Schrein.
5. *Der erste schlug den Schleier zurück,*
   Und schaute sie an mit traurigem Blick.
6. *„Ach lebtest du noch, du schöne Maid!*
   Ich würde dich lieben von dieser Zeit!"
7. *Der zweite deckte den Schleier zu,*
   Und kehrte sich ab, und weinte dazu.
8. *„Ach dass du liegst auf der Todtenbahr!*
   Ich hab' dich geliebet so manches Jahr!"
9. *Der dritte hub den Schleier so gleich,*
   Und küsste sie auf den Mund so bleich.
10. *„Dich liebt' ich immer, dich lieb' ich noch heut',*
    Dich werde ich lieben in Ewigkeit!"

GOOD NIGHT.

1 (Round)
Good night.
2
Slum - - - - - ber sound, In
3
peace pro - - found, Till
4
morn - - ing's light.

DULCE DOMUM.

(Winchester College). 17th Century

Moderato con moto
Voice
Piano
1. Con - ci-na-mus o So - da - les E - ja! quid si - - le - - mus
2. Ap - pro-pin-quat ec - ce! fe - lix Ho - ra gau - di - - o - - rum:
mf
No - bi - le can-ti-cum Dul-ce me-los Do - mum Dul - - ce Do - mum re - - - so - ne-mus.
Post gra-ve tæ-di-um' Ad-ve-nit om-ni - um Me - - ta pe - ti - - ta...... la - bo-rum
p
dim.
CHORUS.
Do - mum, Do - mum, Dul - ce Do - mum, Do - mum, Do - mum, Dul - ce Do - mum
Dul - ce, Dul - ce, Dul - ce Do - mum, Dul - ce Do - mum re - - so - ne - mus.

3. Musa! libros mitte, fessa;
Mitte pensa dura;
Mitte negotium;
Jam datur otium;
Me mea mittito cura.
Chorus.—Domum, Domum, &c.

4. Ridet annus, prata rident:
Nosque rideamus.
Jam repetit Domum
Daulias advena
Nosque Domum repetamus.
Chorus.—Domum, Domum, &c.

5. Heu! Rogere: fer caballos;
Eja! nunc eamus;
Limen amabile,
Matris et oscula,
Suaviter et repetamus.
Chorus.—Domum, Domum, &c.

6. Concinamus ad Penates;
Vox et audiatur:
Phosphore! quid jubar,
Segnius emicans,
Gaudia nostra moratur?
Chorus.—Domum, Domum, &c.

CARMEN LIBERORUM ROMANORUM.

Chorus in unison. 1st time, Andante religioso. 2nd time, Allegro.
Voice
E - ne me - ne mi - ne mo, Car - pe ni - grum di - gi - to;
Piano
Si ex - clam - at sol - ve - to, E - ne me - ne mi - ne mo.

REGIMENTAL SONG OF THE QUEEN'S OWN RIFLES.

Words by Rev. JOHN CAMPBELL, '65. Major F. E. DIXON.

Voice
1. Up, comrades up! 'tis our bu - - - gle, Th'as - sem - bly, it sounds loud and
2. On, comrades on! trav - el fast - - - er; On, not a moment's de-
3. Home, comrades home! ri - fles sling - - - ing, Hearts bounding high with de-
Piano
clear; Of time as in fare let's be fru - - - gal, And
lay; 'Twill bring but dis-grace and dis - as - - - ter, And
light, Flags are fly - ing, the joy bells are ring - - - ing, As they

on with our old fighting gear. Though our feet be sore with the marching, And
make man - y sad hearts to - day. On our quick march perchance are depend - ing Vic-
welcome us home from the fight. Now off to our peaceful vo - ca-tions, The
hun-ger won't leave us a - lone; Though with thirst our lips be
to - ry and the lives of the brave; The quick - er the soon-er its
workshop, the desk, or the gown; We are sure of good quarters and
parching, We're pre - pared! are we not? Queen's Own.
end - ing, And rest comes with peace or the grave.
ra - tions, Till the next time they need the Queen's Own.
CHORUS.
1. Though our feet be sore with the march-ing, And hun - ger won't leave us a -
2. Then though feet be sore with the march-ing, And hun - ger won't leave us a -
3. Now off to our peace-ful vo - ca - tions, The workshop, the desk, or the
lone, Though with thirst our lips be parching, We're prepared! are we not? Queen's Own.
lone, Though with thirst our lips be parching, We will march, will we not? Queen's Own.
gown; We are sure of good quarters and ra-tions. Till the next time they need the Queen's Own.

THOSE EVENING BELLS.

Words by T. MOORE. J. D. KERRISON.

Pathetically.
1. Those even - ing bells, those even - ing bells. How man - y a tale their mus - ic tells Of youth and home and that sweet time When last I heard their soothing chime. Of youth and home and that sweet time When last I heard their soothing chime.
2. Those joy - ous hours are passed a - way, And man - y a heart that then was gay, With - - in the tomb now dark - ly dwells, And hears no more those even-ing bells. With - in the tomb now dark - ly dwells, And hears no more those evening bells.
3. And so 'twill be when I am gone, That tune - ful peal will still ring on, While oth - er bards shall walk these dells, And sing your praise, sweet even-ing bells. While oth - er bards shall walk these dells, And sing your praise, sweet evening bells.
Solemnly.
1. Once on a time there were three little kittens who lived together in a basket of saw - - aw - - - dust.

THREE LITTLE KITTENS.

After 3rd stanza.

Said the first little kitten un-to the two other little cats, "If you don't get out of this Why, I.... must!" That's so!*

2. Now these little kittens (pretty ones) | lived together | in the basket of saw-aw-dust;
Said the second little kitten | unto | the two other little cats,
"If you don't just get out of this, | Why, I *must!*"

3. Still, the three pretty little kittens (such was their imperturbability) | continued to live together | in the basket of saw-aw-dust;
Said the third little kitten | unto | the two other little cats, |
"If you don't just get out of this, | Why, I *shall* Bust!!" That's so.

* With a vigorous nod of affirmation.

THE THREE CROWS.

SOLO.
CHORUS.
SOLO.
1. There were three crows sat on a tree, O Bil-ly Ma-gee Ma-gar! There
2. Said one old crow un-to his mate, O Bil-ly Ma-gee Ma-gar! Said
Billy Magee!

CHORUS.
were three crows sat on a tree, O Billy Magee Magar! There were three crows sat on a tree, And
one old crow un-to his mate, O Billy Magee Magar! Said one old crow unto his mate "What
Billy Magee!

they were black as black could be, And they all flapped their wings and cried Caw, Caw, Caw,
shall we do for grub to ate?" And they all flapped their wings and cried Caw, Caw, Caw,

Bil-ly Magee Magar! And they all flapped their wings and cried Billy Magee Magar!
Bil-ly Magee Magar! And they all flapped their wings and cried Billy Magee Magar!

3. "There lies a horse on yonder plain," } (*bis.*)
Chorus.—O Billy Magee Magar!
"There lies a horse on yonder plain,
Who's by some cruel butcher slain."—*Chorus*

4. "We'll perch ourselves on his backbone," } (*bis.*)
Chorus.—O Billy Magee Magar!
"We'll perch ourselves on his backbone,
"And pick his eyes out one by one."—*Chorus.*

5. "The meat we'll eat before it's stale," } (*bis.*)
Chorus.—O Billy Magee Magar!
"The meat we'll eat before it's stale,
"Till nought remains but bones and tail."—*Chorus.*

* Imitate Crows.

HEIGHO, HEIGHO.

Presto. f
1. As I was walk - ing down the street, Heigh - o, heigh - o, heigh -
2. Said I to her, "What is your trade?" Heigh - o, heigh - o, heigh -
o, heigh - o, A pret - ty girl I chanced to meet, Heigh - o, heigh - o, heigh - o.
o, heigh - o, Said she to me, "I'm a weav - er's maid," Heigho, heigh - o, heigh - o.
Rig - a - jig - jig, and a - way we go, a - way we go, a - way we go,
Rig - a - jig - jig, and a - way we go, a - way we go, a - way we go,
Rig - a - jig - jig, and a - way we go, Heigh - o, heigh - o, heigh - o, heigh-
o, heigh - o, heigh - o, heigh - o, heigh - o, heigh - o, heigh - o, heigh-o,
Rig - a - jig - jig, and a - way we go, Heigh - o, heigh - o, heigh - o.

MARCHING SONG.

Tune—"Heigho Heigho."

Words by J. J. FERGUSON, '90.

1. Come listen to our hearty song,
   Heigho, heigho, heigho, heigho,
 We'll sing it as we march along,
   Heigho, heigho, heigho.

CHORUS.

Rig a jig jig and away we go,
  Heigho, heigho, heigho, heigho,
Rig a jig jig and away we go,
  Heigho, heigho, heigho.

2. Oh! we're the boys of 'Varsity,
 We're out to-night upon a spree.

3. We do our best quite willingly,
 To make Rome howl with melody.

4. We keep the sidewalk two and two,
 Nor turn we out for all the "blue."

5. We hustle them gently out of the way,
 And still we sing our festive lay.

6. They make the hearts of sinners quake,
 And do their duty when awake.

7. We know right well it's very wrong
 To keep the cops awake so long.

8. Good night! next week we'll come again,
 We must inspect them now and then.

THE COLLEGE GOWN.

Tune—"Der Pabst Lebt Herrlich."

Words by REV. J. CAMPBELL, 65.

1. { Oft in the clas-sic page I've read Of Gra - ces three and Mu - ses
Now hea - then dames I bid de - - part, And her my Grace, my Muse, I

rit.
nine, And many a time with ach - ing head. I've begged them to suggest a line
own, She shall in-spire the po - et's heart. She mended my old Col-lege gown.
head, with aching head.
heart, the poet's heart.

2. Dynamic forces ne'er can move
  Th' ecstatic zero of my soul,
 No calculus compute its love,
  Nor optic powers discern the whole.
 Though squared and cubed, no lapse of years
  Can e'er her fond remembrance drown,
 Nay though they numbered thrice the tears
  She mended in my College Gown.

3. No language can express her charms,
  No living tongue her virtues tell;
 Her name the poet's pen disarms,
  And dares his powers to break the spell.
 Nor would he, if he could, disclose
  That name in every language known,
 'Tis stated best in English prose—
  She mended my old College Gown.

4. Philosophy perchance may please
  The earnest and enquiring mind
 But neither mighty Socrates
  Nor Cicero himself could find
 A secret that in ages past
  Baffled sages of renown.
 The *summum bonum*—found at last!
  She mended my old College Gown.

5. Great wonders Science brings to light,
  Great truths her growing powers unfold,
 And Nature spreads before our sight
  A thousand beauties new and old.
 Yet one o'er all I still prefer,
  Who in her kindom wears the crown,
 The world were empty wanting her
  Who mended my old College Gown.

THE BULL-DOG.

Moderato. mf
1. Oh! the bull-dog on the Bank, Oh! the bull-dog on the bank,
2. Oh! the bull-dog stooped to catch him, Oh! the bull-dog stooped to catch him,
And the bull-frog in the pool, And the bull-frog in the pool,
And the snapper caught his paw, And the snapper caught his paw,
rit. ad lib.
CHORUS. Allegro.
Am. Oh! the bull-dog on the bank, And the bull-frog in the pool, The bull - dog called the bull-frog A green old wa - ter fool.
Oh! the bull-dog stooped to catch him, And the snapper caught his paw, The polly - wog died a laughing, To see him wag his jaw.
Sing - ing tra la la la, la la la, Singing tra la la la la la la la. Singing tra la la la la la, Singing tra la la la la la, Tra la la la, tra la la la, tra la la la la la.
leil - i - o, leil - i - o...... leil - i - o
repeat pp

3. Says the monkey to the owl:
"Oh! what'll you have to drink?"
"Why, since you are so very kind,
I'll take a bottle of ink."

4. Oh! the bull-dog in the yard,
And the tom-cat on the roof,
Are practising the Highland Fling,
And singing opera bouffe.

5. Says the tom-cat to the dog,
"Oh! set your ears agog,
For Jule's about to tête-à-tête
With Romeo, *incog.*"

6. Says the bull-dog to the cat
"Oh! what do you think they're at?
They're spooning in the dead of night,
But where's the harm in that?"

7. Pharaoh's daughter on the bank,
Little Moses in the pool,
She fished him out with a telegraph pole
And sent him off to school.

GOOD-NIGHT.

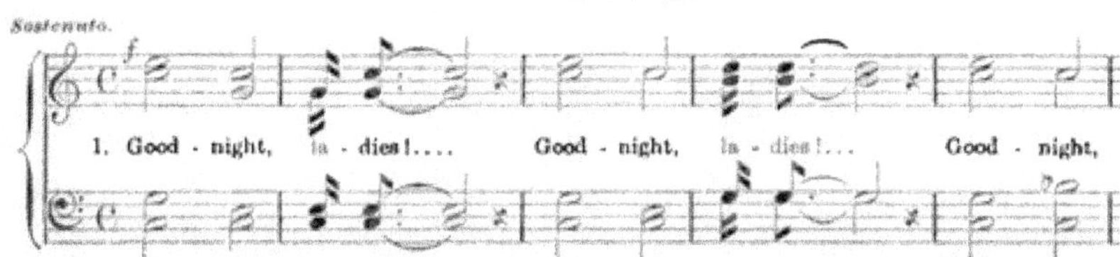
Sostenuto.
f
1. Good - night, la - dies!.... Good - night, la - dies!... Good - night,

Allegro.
la - dies! We're going to leave you now. Mer - ri - ly we roll a-long,

repeat pp
roll a - long, roll a - long, Mer - - ri-ly we roll a - long, O'er the dark blue sea.

2. Farewell, ladies; farewell, ladies;
Farewell, ladies; we're going to leave you now,
Merrily, etc.

3. Sweet dreams, ladies; sweet dreams, ladies;
Sweet dreams, ladies; we're going to leave you now,
Merrily, etc.

MERRILY, MERRILY.

1 (Round.)
2
Mer-ri-ly, mer-ri-ly greet the morn; Cheer-i-ly, cheer-i-ly sound the horn.
3
4
Hark! to the ec-hoes hear them play, O'er hill and dale, far, far, a-way.

SOLOMON LEVI.

FRED SEAVER.

Allegretto.
Voice
Piano
1. My name is Sol-o-mon Le-vi, At my store on Chatham Street, That's
2. And if a bum-mer comes a-long To my store on Chatham Street, And
where you'll buy your coats and vests, And ev-e-ry-thing that's neat; I've se-cond-hand-ed
tries to hang me up for coats And vests so ver-y neat; I kicks the bummer right
Ul-ster-ettes, and everything that's fine, For all the boys they trade with me At a
out of my store And on him sets my pup, For I won't sell clothing to an-y man Who
hundred and for-ty nine.
tries to set me up.
CHORUS in unison.
f
O Sol-o-mon Le-vi! Le-vi! tra la la

la! Poor Sheen - y Le - vi. Tra la la la la la la la la la. My
f
CHORUS.
name is Sol - o - mon Le - vi, At my store on Chatham street; That's where you'll buy your
coats and vests, And ev'rything else that's neat; Se-cond-hand-ed Ulsterettes and
tra la la.
evrything else that's fine, For all the boys they trade with me At a hundred and for-ty-nine.
D.C.

3 The people are delighted to come inside of my store,
And trade with the elegant gentleman what I keeps to walk the floor.
He is a blood among the Sheenies, beloved by one and all,
And his clothes they fit him just like the paper on the wall.—*Chorus.*

PORK, BEANS, AND HARD-TACK;

A REBELLION SONG.

Tune—"Solomon Levi."

1. Our volunteers are soldiers bold, so say the people all,
When duty calls they spring to arms, responsive to the call,
With outfits old and rotten clothes ill-fitted for the strife,
They leave their home on starving pay to take the nitchies' life.

Chorus.

Pork, beans and hard-tack, tra la la la, etc.,
Poor hungry soldier, tra la la, etc.
In rags we march the prairie, most eager for the fray,
But when we near the enemy, they always run away.
As Corporation labourers with fat-i-gue each day,
We dig and scrape and hoe and rake for fifty cents a day.

2. Faint, cold and weary, we're packed on an open car,
Cursing our fate and grumbling as soldiers ever are,
Hungry and thirsty, over the C.P.R. we go
Instead of by the all-rail route—Detroit and Chicago.—*Chorus.*

3. On half cooked beans and fat pork we're fed without relief,
Save when we get a change of grub on hard-tack and corn beef.
On fat-i-gue and guards all day, patrols and pickets by night,
It's thus we while our time away, our duty seems ne'er to fight.

4. Down the wild Saskatchewan in river boats we go,
At last we reach Lake Winnipeg and are taken by a tug in tow.
On board a barge two regiments are shoved into the hold,
Like sardines in a box we're packed, six hundred men all told.

5. Down the length of Winnipeg Lake we roll throughout the night,
And on we're towed along the Lake till Selkirk is in sight,
We disembark in double quick time, we once more board a train.
We're on our way for Winnipeg, we're getting near home again.

6. The ladies of our city are noble dames you know,
And helped us in our woeful plight when grub was very low,
We cannot thank them as we ought for every kindness done,
But we say it from our inmost souls their goodness our hearts has won.

PEGGY MURPHY.

Words and Music by CHARLES M. RYAN.

Voice
1. Oh! swate Peg - - gy Mur - - phy had beau - - ti - ful eyes, They were
Chorus.
Arrah! fal dhe dal, dal dhe dal, dal dhe dal day, Musha!
Piano
dape as two o - ceans, as blue as two skies, And the glan - ces they shot were like
fal dhe dal, dal dhe dal, dal dhe dal -day Ar-rah! fal dhe dal, dal dhe dal

com - ets' big tails, Sure those eyes were quite fit for the Prin - cess of Wales.
dal dhe dal day, Musha! fal dhe dal, dal dhe dal, dal dhe dal day.

2. Her mouth it was like a—och! sure I can't tell,
But whene'er she spoke through it a sound like a bell
Went a ringin' and dingin' straight into my soul,—
Sure a swate little mouth was that same little hole.

3. Her skin it was whiter than newly-laid milk,
And softer by far than the softest of silk;
Her complexion indade was so clear and so fair
You could see through her face all the roots of her hair.

4. Her lips an' her cheeks had an exquisite tint,
So rich and so rare, by the angels 'twas lint;
Arrah! naught could compare with her blushes so red,
When she walked in the garden the roses dropped dead.

5. Her hair was so fine that it couldn't be felt,
An' so much like the sunshine you'd think it would melt;
Oh! it glistened an' dazzled, I'm tellin' no lies,
That to take a look at it you'd shut both your eyes.

6. Her neck an' each shoulder, each arm an' each hand,
Made her fit for a fairy queen holdin' a wand;
Arrah! she was so deservin' of fairy-like things,
I'm not sure but I think she had nice little wings.

7. Her teeth were like pearls strung out in two rows,
Between luscious cherries right under her nose;
They formed a nate fence round such nice private grounds,
Where a sharp teasing tongue never stayed within bounds.

8. Her breath was as pure as a babe's or a dove's,
That milky-like breath that a spoony man loves,
'Twas the clarified essence of nectar an' dew,
An' sugar an' honey made into a stew.

9. For a word or a smile from my paragon Peg
I'd cut off my head, or I'd saw off my leg;
And as for a kiss from her lips fresh and swate,
'Twould so fill me with joy as to intoxicate.

10. I cooed an' I wooed her a year an' a day,
An' I asked her to marry me quick straight away.
Oh! she laughed in my face sayin', "Larry, me boy,
I'm engaged to be married to Mickey McCoy!"

11. Then I threw myself under a willowy tree,
An' I blubbered an' bawled till I scarcely could see.
Why didn't I ask when I first crossed her door
If she'd e'er been engaged or married before?

GAUDEAMUS IGITUR.

1. Gau - de - a - mus i - gi - tur, Ju - ve - nes dum su - mus;
2. U - bi sunt, qui an - te nos, In mun - do fu - e - re?
Gau - de - a - mus i - gi - tur, Ju - ve - nes dum su - mus;
U - bi sunt, qui an - te nos, In mun - do fu - e - re?
Post ju - cun dam ju - ven - tu - tem, Post mo - les - tam se - nec - tu - tem,
Tran - se - as ad su - pe - ros A - be - as ad in - fe - ros,
Nos ha - be - bit hu - - mus, Nos ha - be - bit hu - - - mus.
Quos si vis vi - - de - - - re, Quos si vis vi - - de - - - re.

3. Vita nostra brevis est
   Brevi finietur,
   Venit mors velociter,
   Rapit nos atrociter,
   Nemini parcetur.

4. Vivat academia,
   Vivant professores,
   Vivat membrum quodlibet,
   Vivant membra quælibet
   Semper sint in flore.

5. Vivant omnes virgines
   Faciles, formosæ!
   Vivant et mulieres,
   Teneræ amabiles,
   Bonæ, laboriosæ.

6. Quis confluxus hodie
   Academicorum?
   E longinquo convenerunt
   Protinusque successerunt
   In commune forum.

7. Alma mater floreat,
   Quæ nos educavit,
   Caros et commilitones,
   Dissitas in regiones
   Sparsos, congregavit.

8. Vivat et republica
   Et qui illam regit,
   Vivat nostra civitas,
   Mæcenatum caritas,
   Quæ nos hic protegit.

9. Pereat tristitia
   Pereant osores,
   Pereat diabolus,
   Quivis antiburschius,
   Atque irrisores.

VIVE LA COMPAGNIE.

Words by F. B. HODGINS, '83.

Allegro.
Voice. SOLO.
CHORUS.
1. Bring hither a beak-er and fill it with wine.
Vi - ve la com - pag - nie!
Accomp.
SOLO.
CHORUS.
And pledge Al - ma Ma - ter with nine - ty times nine.
Vi - ve la com - pag - nie!
Vi - ve le, vi - ve le, vi - ve le roi,
Vi - ve le, vi - ve le, vi - ve le roi,
vi - ve le roi, vi - ve la reine,
Vi - ve la com - pag - nie!....

2. Here's to the Senators, all in a row,
But what they are good for I really don't know.

3. The Professors come next, and they're not a bad lot,
There are some that are good, and there are some that are not.

4. Here's to the Ladies—they do as they please,—
Take our places in street-cars and class-lists with ease.

5. Here's to the Freshman, of brazen fifteen,
In his cap and his gown day and night he is seen.

6. Here's to the Bedel, who carries the mace,
As he walks up the aisle he's the model of grace.

7. Here's to the Janitor—here's to the Twins,
You can't tell them apart, they're as like as two pins.

8. Here's to ourselves—we're the best of the crowd,
We're too modest to mention our praises out loud.

9. Here's to the fellow who sings out of tune,
We'll choke him right off, for he can't die too soon.

10. Here's to Exams., but we've drained the last drop,
So I think it is time for this ditty to stop.

OUR NEW DEGREE!

Words by President WILSON — Music by MRS. EDGAR JARVIS.

Piano.
Vivace, mf
dim.
Tempo di Valse.
1. 'Twas at our last Col - - lege
2. The Al - pha - bet took to
3. The Te - to - ta - - lers he
rall.
Vocal or Instrumental Accomp.
la la zum la la zum
din - - - - ner, The text - books fell in - to sad ways, And the
drink - - - ing, And set all the o - thers a - stray,............... First he
ov - - er - hauled., With their W. C. T. U. league,............... And still
old - - est guest so for - got him - self, That he left us all in a
got the big A be - hind the B, And dubbed him - self a B.
worse he be - spat-ter'd the cler - - - - gy, With a B. D. D. D.
maze, in a maze, That he left us all in a maze.
A., a B. A., And dubbed him - self a B. A.
plague, D. D. plague, With a B. D. D. D. plague.

4. He muddled himself so sadly,
That his wits went wildly astray;
Was it LL.D., or L.S.D.,
Or Ph. D., he could not say.

5. Next he led his Roman history
So hopelessly into a scare,
That the common run of P.Q.R.S.
Got blund'ring as S.P.Q.R.

6. He hiccoughed into phonetics,
And slurred every vowel in spite;
And swore he'd reform English spelling,
And give the old Dons such a fright.

7. So at our next convocation
Let the V.C. confer the degree,
And in jolliest nursery fashion
Make him Doctor and A.B.C.

THE BAGPIPES.

Very nasally. W. H. HILLS.

Yi, yi, yi, yi, yi, yi, yi, yi, yi, yi, yi, yi, yi, yi, yi, yi, yi, yi, yi, yi, yi,

Yi, yi, yi, yi, yi, yi, yi, yi, yi, yi, yi, yi, yi, yi, yi, yi, yi......

NOTE.—As the soloist reaches the climax of the swell in the last measure, the chorus, diminuendo-ing, turn on their heels and scatter in all directions, thus illustrating the peculiar die-away dissipation of sound characteristic of the bag-pipes. Meanwhile the soloist, holding his note, stands facing the audience, and puts an added volume of twang into his finish, as though he had, with an effort, squeezed his bag flat.

SAW MY LEG OFF.

Andante. FINE.

ff
Saw my leg off, saw my leg off, saw my leg off, short.

ff
D.C.
Saw my leg off, saw my leg off, saw my leg off, short.

2. Saw it on again, quick.

3. Call your dog off, sharp.

4. Hash for breakfast, Hash for dinner,
Hash for supper, Hash!

* Shouted.

CHINESE SONG.

BARITONE SOLO.
1. Me gettee married, Have a pret - ty wif - ee. Have a pig - gy tail - ee,
2. Me singee songee, Get - ee fiv - ee cent - ee, Tak - ee fiv - ee cent - ee,
Hang it down-ee back, 'Long com - ee Meli - can man. Pull - ee pig - gy tail - ee,
Put him right a - way, 'Long com - ee Meli - can man, Tak - ee fiv - ee cent - ee,
Pull - ee pig - - gy tail - ee Till the face glow black.
Turn - ee right a - round and say, "Hey, what d'ye say."
SOLO
Me lik - ee bow - wow, she lik - ee chow - chow, Me lik - ee lil - lee gal,
CHORUS
Me lik - ee bow - wow, she lik - ee chow - chow Me lik - ee lil - lee gal,
she lik - ee me; 'Long com - ee Meli - can man, pull - ee pig - gy tail - ee,
she lik - ee me; 'Long com - ee Meli - can man, pull - ee pig - gy tail - ee,
Pull - ee pig - - gy tail - ee on the bold Chi - - nee.
Pull - ee pig - - gy tail - ee on the bold Chi - - nee,

THE MERMAID.

Tenors
Basses
Air.
1 'Twas Fri - day morn when we set sail, And we were not far from the land, When the
2. Then up spake the captain of our gallant ship, And a well-spok - en man was he, "I have
Cap - tain spied a love-ly mer-maid, With a comb and a glass in her hand.
mar - ried me a wife in Salem town, And to - night she a wid - dow will be."
CHORUS.
Oh! the o - - cean waves may roll, And the storm - y winds may
blow,............ While we poor sai - lors go skip-ping to the tops, And the
may blow,
land - lubbers lie down be - low, be - low, be-low, And the land - lubbers lie down be - low.

3. Then up spake the cook of our gallant ship,
And a fat old cook was he;
"I care much more for my kettles and my pots,
Than I do for the depths of the sea."—*Chorus.*

4. Then out spake the boy of our gallant ship,
And a well-spoken laddie was he;
"I've a father and mother in Boston city,
But to-night they childless will be."—*Chorus.*

5. "Oh, the moon shines bright and the stars give light;
Oh, my mammy she'll be looking for me;
She may look, she may weep, she may look to the deep,
She may look to the bottom of the sea."—*Chorus.*

6. Then three times around went our gallant ship,
And three times around went she,
Then three times around went our gallant ship,
And she sank to the depths of the sea."—*Chorus.*

UPIDEE.

Yale Version.

1. The shades of night were comin' down swift, U - pi-dee, U - pi-da, The snow was heapin' up drift on drift.

U - pi - dee - i - da, Through a Yan - kee village a youth did go, A - carryin' a flag with this motto.

CHORUS.

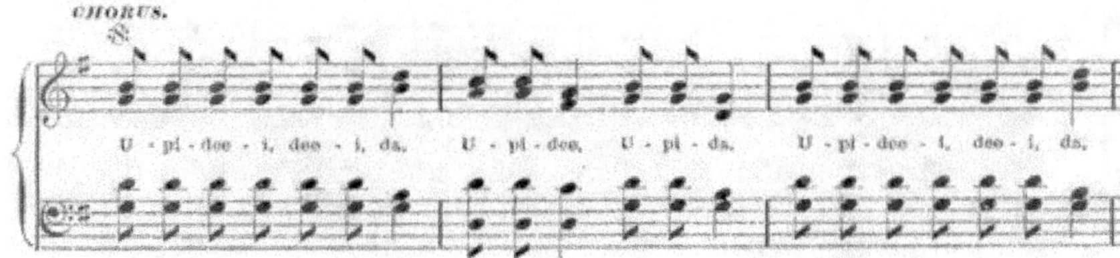
U - pi - dee - i, dee - i, da, U - pi - dee, U - pi - da, U - pi - dee - i, dee - i, da,

FINE.
DAL SEGNO AL FINE.
U - pi - dee - i da!
r-r-r-r - r-r-r-r - r-r-r-r - r-r-r-r - r-r-r-r - r-r-r-r yah! yah! yah! yah!

2. O'er his high forehead curl'd copious hair,
He'd a Roman nose and complexion fair,
He'd a light blue eye and an auburn lash,
And he ever kep' a shoutin' through his moustache.—*Cho*

3. He saw through the windows as he kept gettin' upper,
A number of families sittin' at supper;
But he eyed those slippery rocks very keen,
And fled as he cried, and cried while a-fleein':

4. "O take care you," said the old man, "stop!
It's blowin' gales up there on top;
You'll tumble off on the other side!"
But the hurryin' stranger still replied

5. "O don't go up such a shockin' bad night;
Come sleep on my lap," said a maiden bright.
On his Roman nose a tear-drop come,
But still he remarked, as he upward clumb

6. "Look out for the branch of the sycamore tree!
Dodge rollin' stones if any you see!"
Sayin' which the farmer went to bed,
But the singular voice replied overhead:

7. About a quarter past six the next forenoon,
A man accidentally goin' up soon,
Heard spoken above him, as much as twice,
Those very same words in a very weak voice;

8. Not far, I believe, from a quarter of seven,
He was slow gettin' up, the road bein' uneven,
He found, buried up in the snow and ice,
The boy and his flag with the strange device:

9. He's dead, defunct, without a doubt,
The lamp of his life has entirely gone out;
On the drear hill-side the youth was a-layin'
And there was no more use for him to be a-sayin';

'WAY UP ON THE MOUNTAIN-TOP-TIP-TOP.

Moderato. mf
SOLO
Voice.
Piano.
1. Hark! I hear a voice, 'way up on the mountain-top-tip-top, Descend-ing down below, De-
1st
2nd
scending down below. -scending down below. Let us all.......... unite in love, Trusting
CHORUS
Solo
Let us all unite in love,
in.............. the powers a - bove,.............. Let us - bove,....................
Trust - ing in the powers above, the powers a-bove.
accel.
ritard.
Merrily now we roll, roll, roll, roll, roll, roll, Merrily now we roll, roll, o - ver the deep blue sea.

2. Little Jacky Horner,
A-sitting in a corner,
Eating a Christmas pie;
He stuck in his thumb,
And pulled out a plum,
And said, "What a big boy am I!"
Chorus.—Let us all, etc.

3. Old Mother Hubbard,
She went to the cupboard,
To get her poor dog a bone;
But when she got there,
The cupboard was bare,
And so the poor doggy had none.
Chorus.—Let us all, etc.

MALBROUCK.

Allegretto.
French-Canadian.
Voice.
Piano.
1. Mal-brouck s'en va-t - en guer - - re, Ri too tra la, ri too tra la. Malbrouck s'en va-t - en guer - - re, Ne sait quand re - vien - dra, là bas, Cou-
2. Il re - vien - dra-z - à Pâ - - ques, Ri too tra la, ri too tra la. Il re - vien-dra-z - à Pâ - - ques, Ou à la Tri - ni - té, là bas, Cou-
rall.
ad lib.
a tempo
rit.
CHORUS. a tempo
1st & 2nd Tenor
1st & 2nd Bass
rez, cou - rez, cou - rez! Pe - ti - te fill' jeune et gen - til - - le. Cou - rez, cou - rez, cou - rez! Ven - ez ce soir vous a - mu - ser.......
rall
a tempo.

3. La Trinité se passe,
 Ri too tra la, etc.,
 La Trinité se passe,
 Malbrouck ne revient pas, là bas.

4. Madame à sa tour monte,
 Ri too tra la, etc.,
 Madame à sa tour monte,
 Si haut qu'ell' peut monter, là bas.

5. Elle aperçoit son page,
 Ri too tra la, etc.
 Elle aperçoit son page
 Tout de noir habillé, là bas.

6. "Beau page, ah! mon beau page,
 Quell' nouvelle apportez?"

7. "Aux nouvell's que j'apporte,
 Vos beaux yeux vont pleurer.

8. Quittez vos habits roses,
 Et vos satins brochés.

9. Monsieur Malbrouck est more,
 Est mort et enterré.

10. J'l'ai vu porter en terre,
 Par quatre-z-officiers."

HONOUR OLD 'VARSITY.

Words adapted by E. C. ACHESON, '89.
NORWEGIAN NATIONAL AIR.—"SONNER AF NORGE."
PIANO.
1st & 2nd Tenor.
f
1. Minstrel awaken the harp from its slumbers, Joyfully strike for the
f
Bass.
old 'Varsity! High and hero - ic in soul-stirring numbers, Dear Alma Mater, we strike it for thee.
mf
Old re - col - lec - tions wake our af - fec - - tions, Each time we speak of the
mf
f
days that are past; Hearts beating loudly and cheeks glowing proudly, Honour old 'Varsity and will to the last.
f

2. Wide now are scattered thy sons and thy daughters,—
   Oft, when begin the long shadows to fall,
On us, in floods, like the swift, rushing waters,
   Crowd recollections of hours past recall.
Days full of pleasure without stint or measure,—
   Days when the hours were like birds on the wing,
These were our blessing, when, ardor possessing,
   Dwelt we at 'Varsity, whose praise now we sing.

3. Minstrel, awaken the harp from its slumbers,
   Joyfully strike for the old 'Varsity!
High and heroic, in soul stirring numbers,
   Dear Alma Mater, we strike it for thee.
Heedless of others, maidens and brothers,
   Stick to your colors with hearts brave and free,
Aid freely lend her, and stoutly defend her,
   Honour old 'Varsity, dear 'Varsity.

ALMA MATER.

TUNE.—"AN DER SAALE HELLEM STRANDE." Words by PRESIDENT WILSON.

Andante.
Comrades, brothers in the bat - tle Of an ar-duous strife and long, Join we
heart and hand while here we Laud our Col-lege life in song, Laud our Col-lege life in song.

2. Life is earnest; be our purpose
Here to win its noblest prize;
Hold on high the lamp of learning,
Emulate the great and wise.

3. Seize the rich award that culture
Offers in the generous strife;
Win and wear it as the guerdon
Of a pure and noble life.

4. Press still onward in th' arena,
Emulation needs no spur;
Hold the honor of our College
High above detraction's slur.

5. Till the day our Alma Mater
Crowns each victor in the fight;
Then to wear her laurels proudly,
And may God defend the right!

COMMENCEMENT.

TUNE—"DEUTSCHES WEINELIED." Words by President WILSON.

And are they done, those hal - cyon days, Those years of toil and
plea - sure That bound us to our Col-lege Halls? Too ill ex-changed for lei - - sure.

2. Familiar scenes of rainbow hope
And cordial emulation;
Of matches on the College lawn,
And speeches on the nation!

3. Of Locke and Hegel, Comte and Kant,
Of Jelf upon the Article;
Or, for a treat, a grind at Tait's
Dynamics of a Particle!

4. The genial converse, social cheer
Of friendship, true as tender;
With rivals in the generous strife
For Fame, and no surrender.

5. Farewell, ye dear old College joys!
'Tis in some novel sense meant
This ending of life's jolliest days,
And calling it Commencement!

Miscellaneous.

SAIL, SAIL, MY BARK CANOE.

Air.—"Pif, Paf"
F. E. SEYMOUR, '94.
Voice.
Piano
1. Where the pine tree wav - eth, And the lake-let blue Rock - y beaches lav - eth, Sail our merry crew. In our island dwell - ing We make hol - i day; Joys beyond all tell - ing Ban-ish care a - way.
2. When the sun is sink - ing 'Neath the lof - ty pines, We of dinner think - ing, Take our hooks and lines, Slow-ly past the rocky shore Troll we, not in vain. With pick - er - el and bass galore We hasten back a - gain.
CHORUS.
Sail, sail, my bark ca-noe, O'er Jo-seph's wa-ters blue! Haste to the kind and true,

Ere daylight's o'er....... Sail, sail, my skiff so light! Sail, sail, for the

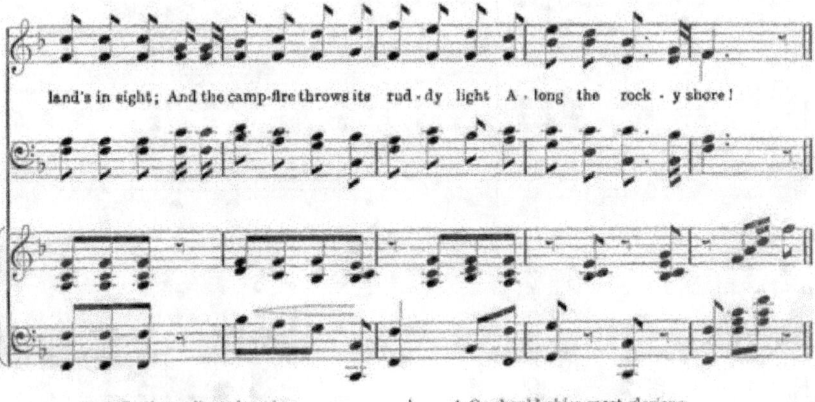

land's in sight; And the camp-fire throws its rud-dy light A-long the rock-y shore!

3. In the mellow gloaming
Rings our dinner bell;
Weary with our roaming,
We like the sound full well.
And when we've done our dining,
In kilmarnocks bright
Round the fire reclining,
We spend a jolly night.

4. Or should skies most glorious,
Tempt once more to stray,
Moonbeams dancing o'er us,
Light each rock-bound bay;
Maidens fair, with eyes of light,
Freight our shallops frail;
And far beneath the Queen of Night
We merrily sing and sail.

THE TARPAULIN JACKET.

Moderato e tranquillo.
Voice.
1. A tall stal-wart Lan-cer lay dy-ing, And
Piano
p

as on his deathbed he lay,............ To his friends who a-round him were
sighing, These last dy-ing words he did say...............
CHORUS. mf
Wrap me up in my tar-pau-lin jac-ket, jac-ket, And say a poor
p
mf
rit. e dim.
a tempo
buff-er lies low, lies low, And six stal-wart Lan-cers shall carry me,
p
mf
dim.
car-ry me, With steps so-lemn, mourn-ful, and slow...........

2. Had I the wings of a little dove,
Far, far away would I fly,
Straight to the arms of my true love,
There would I lay me and die.
Chorus.—Wrap me up, &c.

3. Then get you two little white tombstones,
Put them one at my head and my toe,
And get you a pen-knife and scratch there
"Here lies a poor buffer below."
Chorus.—Wrap me up, &c.

4. And get you six brandies and sodas,
And lay them all out in a row,
And get you six jolly good fellows,
To drink to this buffer below.
Chorus.—Wrap me up, &c.

5. And then in the calm of the twilight,
When the soft winds whispering blow,
And the darkening shadows are falling,
Sometimes think of this buffer below.
Chorus.—Wrap me up, &c.

BONNIE DOON.

Words by BURNS, 1792.
Tune.—"Lost is my Quiet forever."
1. Ye banks and braes of bon - nie Doon, How can ye bloom sae fresh and fair How
2. Oft have I strayed by bon - nie Doon, To see the rose and woodbine twine; Where
can ye chaunt ye lit - tle birds, And I sae wea - ry, full of care? You'll
il - ka bird sang o' his love, And fond - ly sae did I of mine, With
break my heart ye lit - tle birds, That wan - ton through the flow'r ing thorn: Ye
lightsome heart I pulled a rose, Full sweet up - on its thorn y tree; But
mind me of de - part - ed joys, De - part - ed, nev - er to re - turn.
my false lov - er stole the rose, And left the thorn be - hind to me

AULD LANG SYNE.

Tune.—Vide Page 21. BURNS.

1. Should auld acquaintance be forgot,
   And never brought to min'?
   Should auld acquaintance be forgot,
   And days o' lang syne?

2. We twa ha'e run aboot the braes,
   And pu'd the gowans fine;
   But we've wandered mony a weary foot,
   Sin' auld lang syne.

3. We twa ha'e paidl't i' the burn
   Frae mornin' sun till dine;
   But seas between us braid ha'e roared,
   Sin' auld lang syne.

4. Then here's a hand, my trusty frien',
   And gie's a hand o' thine,
   And we'll tak' a cup o' kindness yet
   For auld lang syne.

Chorus.

For auld lang syne, my dear,
For auld lang syne;
We'll tak' a cup o' kindness yet
For auld lang syne.

TENTING ON THE OLD CAMP GROUND.

Tempo di marcia.

Words and Music by WALTER KITTREDGE.

Voice.

Piano.

1. We're tent - ing to - night on the old Camp ground, Give us a song to cheer Our wea - ry hearts, a song of home, And friends we love so dear.
2. We've been tent - ing to - night on the old Camp ground, Thinking of days gone by, Of the lov'd ones at home that gave us the hand, And the tear that said "Good-bye!"
3. We're tired of war on the old Camp ground, Man - y are dead and gone Of the brave and true who've left their homes, Others been wounded long.
4. We've been fight - ing to - day on the old Camp ground, Man - y are ly - ing near; Some are dead and some are dy - ing, Many are in tears.

CHORUS.

Many are the hearts that are weary to-night, Wishing for the war to cease, Man - y are the hearts looking for the right, To see the dawn of peace.

Tenting to-night, Tenting to-night, Tenting on the old Camp ground.

pp Last verse. (*lento*). *ppp*

Dy - ing to-night, Dy - ing to-night, Dy - ing on the old Camp ground.

DIE LORELEI.

HEINE, 1823. SILCHER.

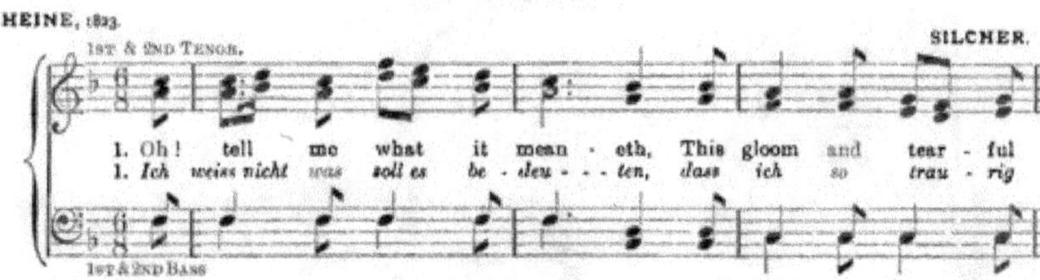
1st & 2nd Tenor.
1. Oh! tell me what it mean - eth, This gloom and tear - ful
1. Ich weiss nicht was soll es be - deu - - - ten, dass ich so trau - rig
1st & 2nd Bass

eye?.... 'Tis mem - o - ry that re - tain - eth The tale of years gone
bin...... Ein Mährchen aus al - ten - Zei - ten, das kommt mir nicht aus dem

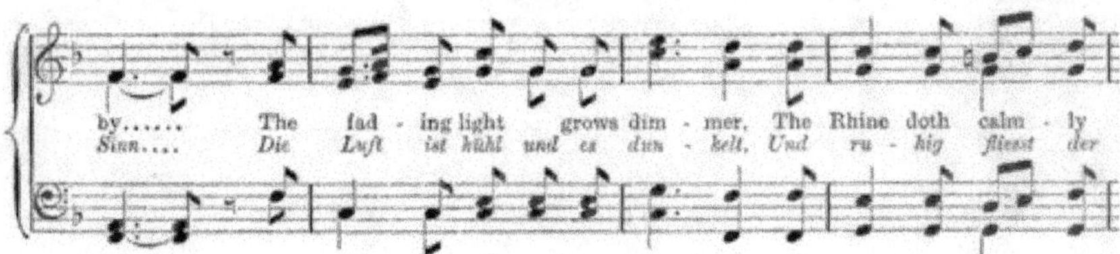
by...... The fad - ing light grows dim - mer, The Rhine doth calm - ly
Sinn.... Die Luft ist kühl und es dun - kelt, Und ru - hig fliesst der

flow,......... The lof - ty hill - tops glim - mer Red with the sun - set glow.....
Rhein......... Der Gipfel des Ber - ges fun - kelt, Im A - bend - son - nen-schein....

2. Above the maiden sitteth,
   A wondrous form and fair;
With jewels bright she plaiteth
   Her shining golden hair:
With comb of gold prepares it,
   The task with song beguiled;
A fitful burden bears it—
   That melody so wild.

3. The boatman on the river,
   Lists to the song, spell-bound;
Oh! what shall him deliver
   From danger threat'ning 'round?
The waters deep have caught them,
   Both boat and boatman brave;
The Loreley's song hath brought them
   Beneath the foaming wave.

2. *Die schönste Jungfrau sitzet*
   Dort oben wunderbar,
Ihr goldnes Geschmeide blitzet
   Sie kämmt ihr goldnes Haar.
Sie kämmt es mit goldenem Kamme
   Und singt ein Lied dabei
Das hat eine wundersame
   Gewaltige Melodei.

3. *Den Schiffer im kleinen Schiffe*
   Ergreift es mit wildem Weh;
Er schaut nicht die Felsenriffe,
   Er sieht nur hinauf in die Höh'
Ich glaube, die Wellen verschlingen
   Am Ende Schiffer und Kahn;
Und das hat mit ihrem Singen
   Die Lorelei gethan.

OLD BLACK JOE.

Poco adagio.
Words and Music by STEPHEN C. FOSTER.
Voice.
Piano.
1. Gone are the days when my heart was young and gay, Gone are my friends from the cot - ton fields a - way, Gone from the earth to a bet - ter land I know, I hear their gen-tle voi - ces call-ing "Old Black Joe."
2. Why should I weep when my heart should feel no pain? Why do I sigh that my friends come not a - gain, Griev - ing for forms now de - part - ed long a - go? I
3. Where are the hearts once so hap - py and so free? The chil - dren so dear that I held up - on my knee, Gone to the shore where my soul has long'd to go, I
Chorus.
I'm com-ing, I'm com-ing, For my head is bend-ing low; I hear their gen - tle voi - ces call-ing "Old Black Joe."

ROSALIE.

Moderato.
Voice
Piano
1. Je suis Pierre le bon - ton de Pa - ris, de Pa - ris, I
2. At the fête de Ma - dame la Mar - quise, la Mar - quise, I
3. Je suis le grand beau de Pa - ris, de Pa - ris, I'm
drink the di - vine eau de vie, eau de vie, I drive in the Bois in my
first felt e - nough at my ease, at my ease, To go to her père and de -
called by les dames très jol - i, très jol - i, When I go out of doors my
poco rit.
lit - tle cou - - pé, And I tell you I'm something to see.
mand for my own, The hand of my sweet Ros - - a - - lie.
friends by the scores, Say "Com - ment ça va mon a - - mi."
a tempo
I care not what others may say, I'm in

love with my Ros - - a - lie.................. Sweet Rose.............. Lit - tle

poco rall.

Rose.............. I'm in love with my Ros - - a - lie.

Last verse. And my Rose is in love with me.

colla voce.

CHORUS.

1st Tenor. *mf*

Air.

I care................ not what o - thers may say. I'm in

1st Bass.

2nd Bass.

love with my Ros - a - lie............ Sweet Rose. *Jol - ie*

rit.

Rose.............. I'm in love with my Ros a - lie.

Last verse. And my Rose is in love with me.

KINGDOM COMING.

Allegro.
Words and Music by HENRY C. WORK.
Voice.
Piano.
1. Say, dar - keys hab you seen de mas - sa, Wid de muff - stash on his
2. He six foot one way, 'two foot tud - der, An' he weigh tree hun - dred
face, Go long de road some time dis mornin', Like he gwin to leab de place? He
pound His coat so big, he couldn't pay de tailor, An' it won't go half way round. He
seen a smoke, way up de ribber, Whar de Link-um gun - boats lay; He
drill so much dey call him Cap'an, An' he get so dref - ful tanned, I
took his hat, an' lef ber-ry sud-den, An' I spec he's run a - way!
spec he try and fool dem Yan-kees For to tink he's con - tra - band!

CHORUS.
De mas - sa run, ha, ha! De dar - keys stay, ho, ho! It
mus' be now de king - dom com-in', An' de year of Ju - bi - lo!

3. De darkeys feel so lonesome, libing
In de log-house on de lawn,
Dey move dar tings to massa's parlor,
For to keep it while he's gone.
Dar's wine an' cider in de kitchen,
An' de darkeys dey'll hab some;
I spose dey'll all be cornfiscated
When de Linkum sojers come.—*Chorus.*

4. De oberseer he make us trouble,
An' he dribe us round a spell;
We lock him up in de smoke-house cellar,
Wid de key trown in de well.
De whip is lost, de han'cuff broken,
But de massa'll hab his pay;
He's ole enough, big enough, ought to known better,
Dan to went an' run away.—*Chorus.*

THE TWO ROSES.

Andante. mf WERNER.

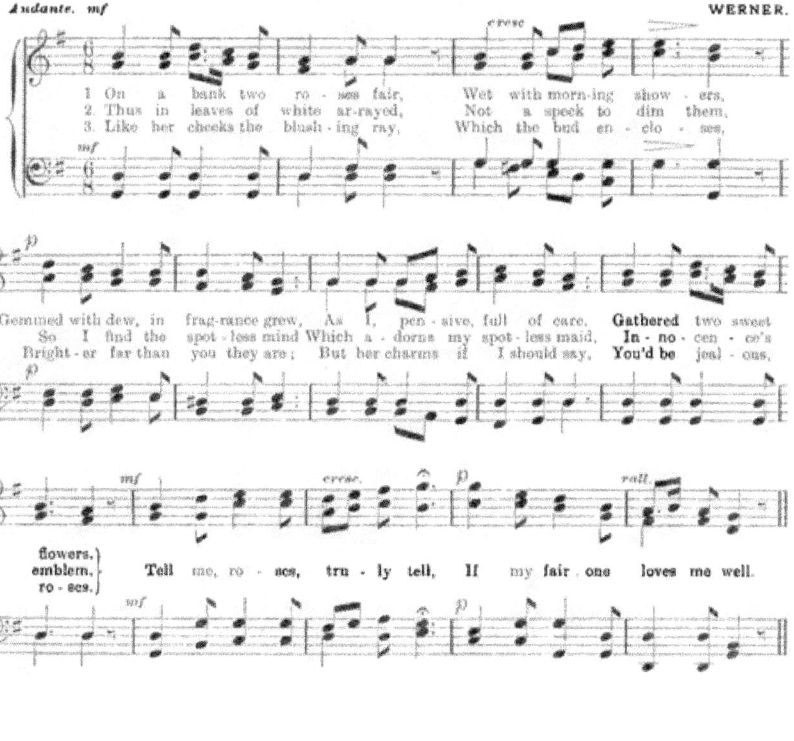

1 On a bank two ro - ses fair, Wet with morn-ing show - ers,
2. Thus in leaves of white ar-rayed, Not a speck to dim them,
3. Like her cheeks the blush - ing ray, Which the bud en - clo - ses,

Gemmed with dew, in frag-rance grew, As I, pen - sive, full of care, Gathered two sweet flowers.
So I find the spot - less mind Which a - dorns my spot - less maid, In - no - cen - ce's emblem.
Bright - er far than you they are; But her charms if I should say, You'd be jeal - ous, ro - ses.

Tell me, ro - ses, tru - ly tell, If my fair one loves me well.

THE POACHERS OF LINCOLNSHIRE.

Allegro.
Old English.
Voice
Piano
1. When I was bound ap - pren - - - tice In fa - - mous Lin - coln-
shire,........ I served my mas - ter faith - ful - ly, For more than sev - en
year, Till I took up to poach - - ing, As you shall quick - ly hear.
cres.
CHORUS. All parts in unison.
1st
2nd
For 'tis my delight of a shin - y night, in the sea - son of the year! year.

2. As me and my companions were setting of a snare,
'Twas then we spied the gamekeeper—for him we didn't care;
For we can wrestle and fight my boys, jump over anywhere,—
For 'tis my delight of a shiny night, in the season of the year!

3. As me and my companions were setting four and five,
And taking of them up again, we took the hare alive;
We popped her into a bag, my boys, and thro' the wood did steer,—
For 'tis my delight of a shiny night, in the season of the year!

4. I threw her on my shoulders, and wandered through the town,
We took her to a neighbor's house, and sold her for a crown;
We sold her for a crown, my boys, but I didn't tell you where,—
For 'tis my delight of a shiny night, in the season of the year!

5. Success to every gentleman who lives in Lincolnshire,
Success to every poacher that wants to sell a hare;
Bad luck to every gamekeeper that will not sell his deer,—
For 'tis my delight of a shiny night, in the season of the year!

OLD FOLKS AT HOME.

Moderato.
S. C. FOSTER.
1st Tenor.
Air.
1. Way down up - on de Swa - nee Rib - ber, Far, far a - way,
2. All round de lit - tle farm I wan-dered When I was young,
3. One lit - tle hut a - mong de bush - es, One dat I love,
1st Bass.
2nd Bass.
Dere's where my heart is turn - ing eb - ber. Dere's where de old folks stay.
Den ma - ny hap - py day I squan-dered, Ma - ny de songs I sung,
Still sad - ly to my mem - 'ry rush - es, No mat - ter where I rove,
All up and down de whole cre - a - t'on, Sad - ly I roam.
When I was play - ing wid my brud-der, Hap - py was I,
When shall I see de bees a - hum-ming All round de comb?
FINE.
Still long - ing for de old plant - a - tion, And for de old folks at home.
Oh! take me to my kind old mud - der. Dere let me lib and die.
When shall I hear de ban - jo thrum-ming, Down in my good old home?
FINE.
ref. O dar - keys, how my heart grows wear - y, Far from the old folks at home.
Dal Segno al Fine.
Ref. All de world am sad and drear - y, Eb - ry where I roam,

CAMPING SONG.

Words by W. H. ELLIS, '67.
Tune.—"WANDERLIED."
VOICES.
PIANO.
1. We have left far be - hind us the dwell - ings of men, We have
2. On the lone rug - ged rocks a rich ta - ble we spread, The
3. When the or - i - ent hues of the dawn - ing of day, Em-
tra - versed the for - est, the lake and the fen; From is - land to
moss and the brac-ken af - ford us a bed; While the gleam of our
bla - zon the clouds and smile back from the bay, We spring from our
is - land like sea - birds we roam, The waves are our path, and the
camp-fire il - lu - mines the sky, And the mur-mur - ing pines sing a
couch like the stag from his lair, And drink in new life with the
world is our home, From is - land to is - land like sea - birds we
soft lul - la - by. While the gleam of our camp - fire il - lu - mines the
free morn-ing air. We spring from our couch like a stag from his

f
roam, The waves are our path, and the world is our home, is our home.
sky, And the murmur - ing pines sing a soft lul - la - - by, lul - la - by.
lair, And drink in new life with the fresh morn-ing air, morning air.

CHORUS. mf
1ST & 2ND TENORS.
Ju - vi - - val - le - ra, Ju - vi - - val - le - ra. Ju - vi - - val - le - ral - le - ral - le-
BASS. mf

f
rall.
ra! Ju - vi - val - le-ra, Ju - vi - val - le - ra, Ju - vi - val - - le - ral - le-ral - le - ra!

4. Then we launch our light bark on the silvery lake,
That dimples and breaks into smiles in our wake;
While we sweeten our toil with a tale or a song,
Or rest while the winds waft us bravely along.

Juvivallera, &c.

5. At night when the deer to the thicket has fled,
And the scream of the nighthawk is heard overhead,
We startle with laughter the wilderness dim,
Or the forests resound with our evening hymn.

Juvivallera, &c.

6. Then hurrah for the north, with its woods and its hills!
Hurrah for its rocks, and its lakes, and its rills!
And long may its forests be lovely as now,
Untouched by the axe and unscathed by the plow!

Juvivallera, &c.

THE VICAR OF BRAY.

Marcato.
17th Century.
Voice.
Piano.
1. In good King Charles's gold - en days, When loy - al - ty no harm meant, A
2. When roy - al James ob-tained the crown, And Pop-'ry came in fa - shion, The
zea - lous High Churchman was I, And so I got pre - fer - - ment; To
pe - - nal laws I hoot - ed down, And read the De - clar - - a - - tion; The
teach my flock I nev - - er missed, Kings were by God ap - point - - ed, And
Church of Rome I found would fit Full well my con - sti - - tu - - tion; And
damn'd are those who do re - sist, Or touch the Lord's a - - - noint - - ed
had be - come a Je - su - it, But for the Re - vo - - - - lu - - tion.

CHORUS.
And this is law, I will maintain, Un - til my dy - ing day, Sir, That what-so ev - er
King may reign, Still I'll be the Vicar of Bray, Sir.
PIANO.

3. When William was our King declared,
To ease a nation's grievance,
With this new wind about I steered,
And swore to him allegiance;
Old principles I did revoke,
Set conscience at a distance;
Passive obedience was a joke,
A jest was non-resistance.
And this is law, &c.

4. When gracious Anne became our Queen,
The Church of England's glory,
Another face of things was seen,
And I became a Tory;
Occasional Conformists base,
I damn'd their moderation,
And thought the Church in danger was,
By such prevarication.
And this is law, &c.

5. When George in pudding time came o'er,
And moderate men looked big, sir,
I turned a cat-in-a-pan once more,
And so became a Whig, sir;
And thus, preferment I procured,
From our new faith's defender,
And almost every day abjured
The Pope and the Pretender.
And this is law, &c.

6. The illustrious house of Hanover,
And Protestant succession,
To these I do allegiance swear,
While they can keep profession—
For in my faith and loyalty
I never more will falter,
And George my lawful King shall be,
Until the times do alter.
And this is law, &c.

THE YOUNG RECRUIT.*

Allegretto. In unison.
ARRANGED FOR MALE VOICES FROM KÜCKEN.
VOICE.
1. See these rib - - - bons gay - - ly stream - - - - - ing, I'm a sol - dier now, Li - zette, I'm a sol - dier now, Li - zette, And of bat - tle
2. We will march a - - way to - - mor - - - - - row, At the break-ing of the day. At the break - ing of the day, And the trum - pets
3. Shame, Lizette, to still be weep - - - - - ing, While there's fame in store for me, While there's fame in store for me, Think when home I
PIANO.
cresc.

* By permission of Messrs. ROBERT COCKS & Co., London.

I am dream - - - ing, And the hon - or I shall get.
will be sound - - - ing, And the mer - ry cym - - bals play.
am re - - turn - - - ing, What a joy - ful day 'twill be.
f
1st Tenor.
Air.
With a sa - bre at my side, And a hel-met on my brow, And a proud steed to
Yet be - fore I say good-bye, And a last sad parting take, As a proof of your
When to church you're fondly led, Like some la - dy smartly dressed, And a he-ro you shall
1st Bass.
2nd Bass.
ride, I shall rush on the foe, Yes, I flat - ter me, Lizette, 'Tis a life that well will
love, Wear this gift for my sake. Then cheer up, my own Lizette, Let not grief your beauty
wed, With a medal on his breast. Ha! there's not a maiden fair, But with welcome will sa-

cresc.
suit The gay life of a young re - - cruit.................. The gay life of a
stain; Soon you'll see your re - cruit a - - gain.................. Soon you'll see your re -
lute The gay bride of the young re - - cruit.................. The gay bride of the
mf.
cresc.
f
young re - cruit..............
cruit a - gain..............
young re - cruit..............
De-rum, De-rum, drum, drum, drum. drum..........
drum..........................drum, drum,
drum, drum
semper staccato
.... Think of me love in your dream - - ing, De-rum, de-rum, drum,
drum............
staccato

drum, drum, drum.............. And the mean - ing of my drum!..............
drum, drum, drum.

MASSA'S IN THE COLD GROUND.

Poco lento.

Words and Music by S. C. FOSTER.

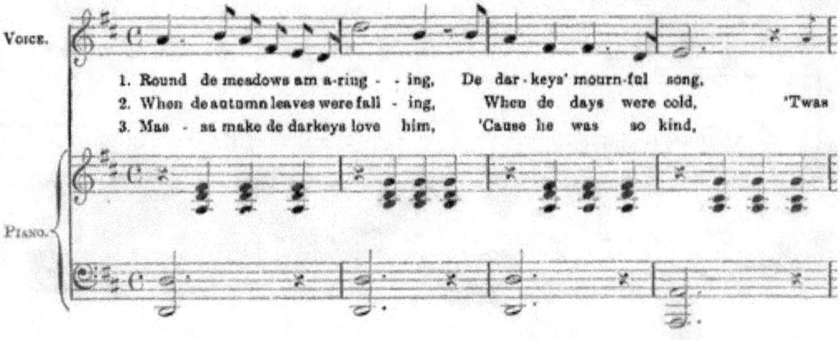

Voice.

1. Round de meadows am a-ring - - ing, De dar - keys' mourn-ful song,
2. When de autumn leaves were fall - ing, When de days were cold, 'Twas
3. Mas - sa make de darkeys love him, 'Cause he was so kind,

Piano.

While de mocking-bird am sing - - ing, Hap-py as de day am long.
hard to hear old massa call - - ing, Cause he was so weak and old.
Now dey sad-ly weep a - bove him, Mourning 'cause he leave dem behind. I

Where de i-vy am a-creep---ing, O'er de grass-y mound,
Now de orange tree am bloom--ing, On de sand-y shore,
can--not work before to-mor--row, 'Cause de tear-drop flow, I
Dare ole massa am a-sleep--ing, Sleeping in de cold, cold ground.
Now de summer days are com--ing, Mas-sa nebber calls no more.
try to drive a-way my sor--row, Pick-in' on de old ban--jo.
CHORUS.
1st & 2nd Voices.
Down in de corn--field, Hear dat mourn-ful sound,
All the darkeys am a-weep--ing, Massa's in de cold, cold ground.

A CAPITAL SHIP. *

SOLO
Arranged for Male Voices.
VOICE.
PIANO.
1. A cap-i-tal ship for an o-cean trip Was the Wallop-ing Win-dow Blind. No wind that blew dismayed her crew, Or troubled the cap-tain's mind. The man at the wheel was made to feel Con-tempt for the wildest blow-ow-ow, Though it often ap-peared, when the gale had cleared, That he'd been in his bunk be-low.
2. The bo'ewain's mate was very se-date, Yet fond of a-muse-ment too; He played hop-scotch with the starboard watch, While the captain he tickled the crew! And the gunner we had was ap-parent-ly mad, For he sat on the af-ter ra-ai-ail, And fired sa-lutes with the cap-tain's boots, In the teeth of the boom-ing gale.
3. The cap-tain sat on the commodore's hat, And dined in a roy-al way Off toast-ed pigs and pickles and figs And gunnery bread each day. And the cook was Dutch, and behaved as such; For the diet he gave the crew-ew-ew, Was a number of tons of hot cross buns Served up with su-gar and glue.

*By permission of Mr. JOHN BLOCKLEY, London, Eng.

CHORUS.
1st Tenor.
Air.
2nd Bass.
Marcato.
Then blow, ye winds, heigh-ho! A - rov - ing I will go! I'll stay no more on
England's shore, So let the mu - sic play - ay - ay! I'm off for the morning train! I'll
cross the raging main! I'm off to my love with a boxing-glove, Ten thousand miles a - way!

4. All nautical pride we laid aside,
And we ran the vessel ashore
On the Gulliby Isles, where the Poopoo smiles,
And the rubbly Ubdugs roar.
And we sat on the edge of a sandy ledge,
And shot at the whistling bee-ee-ee;
And the cinnamon bats wore waterproof hats
As they dipped in the shiny sea.—*Chorus.*

5. On Rugbug bark, from morn till dark,
We dined till we all had grown
Uncommonly shrunk; when a Chinese junk
Came up from the Torriby Zone.
She was chubby and square, but we didn't much care,
So we cheerily put to sea-ee-ee;
And we left all the crew of the junk to chew
On the bark of the Rugbug tree.—*Chorus.*

DRINK TO ME ONLY.
Words by BEN. JONSON.
Harmonized by THEO. MARTENS.
Slowly.
1. Drink to me on - - ly with thine eyes, And I will pledge with mine ;......
2. I sent thee late a ro - sy wreath, Not so much hon 'ring thee,......
AIR
Or leave a kiss with - in the cup, And I'll not ask for wine ;.... The
As giv-ing it a hope that there It could not with - er'd be ;.... But
AIR
thirst that from the soul doth rise, Doth ask a drink di - - vine,......
thou there-on didst on - ly breathe, And sent'st it back to me,......
But might I of Love's nec - tar sip, I would not change for thine.
Since when it grows, and smells, I swear, Not of it - self, but thee.
AIR
A CANADIAN BOAT SONG.
Andante.
THOMAS MOORE.
1. Faintly as tolls the ev'ning chime, Our voices keep tune and our oars keep time,.... Our
2. Why should we yet our sail un-furl ? There is not a breath the blue wave to curl,.... There
3. Ot - ta - wa tide ! this trembling moon Shall see us float o - ver thy sur - ges soon,.... Shall
voi - ces keep tune and our oars keep time. Soon as the woods on shore look dim, We'll
is not a breath the blue wave to curl, But when the wind blows off the shore, Oh,
see us float o - ver thy sur - ges soon. Saint of this green isle, hear our prayer.

cres - - cen - - do. dim tr f sf f
sing at St. Ann's our part - ing hymn. Row, brothers, row, the stream runs fast, The
sweet-ly we'll rest our wea - ry oar. Blow, breezes, blow, the stream runs fast, The
Grant us cool heav'ns and fav - 'ring air. Blow, breezes, blow, the stream runs fast, The
f dim. f sf dim.
rapids are near and the day-light's past, The rapids are near and the day - light's past.

STARS TREMBLING O'ER US.

Andante. D. M. MULOCH.

1. Stars trem-bling o'er us, And sun - set be - fore us, Moun - tain in shad-ow and
2. Come not, pale Sor-row, Flee, flee till to - mor - row, Rest soft - ly fall - ing o'er
3. As the waves cov - er The depths we glide o - ver So let the past in for-

for - est a - sleep.
eye - lids that weep;
get - ful - ness sleep,
} Down the dim riv - er We float on for - ev - er, Speak not, ah,

breathe not! there's peace on the deep, Speak not, ah, breathe not! there's peace on the deep.

JOHNNY SCHMOKER.

In this song, an old German musician tells his friend, Johnny Schmoker, about the instruments upon which he can play, and describes them by motions while he sings. The motions are made only when the words describing the instruments are sung, as, for example, at "Rub, a dub, a dub," the roll of the drum is imitated, beginning—as in the case of all the instruments—with the first and ending exactly with the last word. At "Pilly, willy, wink," the hands are placed as if playing the fife, and only the fingers move; at "Tic, knock, knock," the right hand strikes three times under the left, as if playing the triangle; at "Bom, bom, bom," the hand is moved forward and back, as if playing the trombone; and so on to the last, which is imitated by crooking both arms and striking with them against the sides, as if playing the bagpipe.

Allegretto.
G. F. ROOT.
1. John - ny Schmo-ker, John - ny Schmo-ker, Ich kann spiel - en, ich kann
2. John - ny Schmo-ker, John - ny Schmo-ker, Ich kann spiel - en, ich kann
spiel - en, Ich kann spiel mein klei - ne Drummel.
spiel - en, Ich kann spiel mein klei - ne
1st.
Rub a dub a dub, das ist mein
2nd.
Drummel.
Fi - fie. Pilly willy wink, das ist mein Fi - fie. Rub a dub a dub, das ist mein
Drummel. Mein Rub a dub a dub, mein Pilly willy wink, Das ist mein Fi - fie.

3. Johnny Schmoker, Johnny Schmoker,
Ich kann spielen, ich kann spielen,
Ich kann spiel mein klein Triangle.
Tic knock knock, das ist Triangle.
Pilly willy wink, das ist mein Fifie,
Rub a dub a dub, das ist mein Drummel.
Mein Rub a dub a dub, mein Pilly willy wink,
Mein Tic knock knock, das ist Triangle.

4. Johnny Schmoker, Johnny Schmoker,
Ich kann spielen, ich kann spielen,
Ich kann spiel mein kleine Trombone.

Bom bom bom, das ist mein Trombone,
Tic knock knock, das ist Triangle,
Pilly willy wink, das ist mein Fifie,
Rub a dub a dub, das ist mein Drummel.
Mein Rub a dub a dub, mein Pilly willy wink,
Mein Tic knock knock, mein Bom bom bom,
Das ist mein Trombone.

5 Johnny Schmoker, Johnny Schmoker,
Ich kann spielen, ich kann spielen,
Ich kann spiel mein kleine Cymbal.
Zoom zoom zoom, das ist mein Cymbal,
Bom bom bom, das ist mein Trombone,
Tic knock knock, das ist Triangle,
Pilly willy wink, das ist mein Fifie,
Rub a dub a dub, das ist mein Drummel.
Mein Rub a dub a dub, mein Pilly willy wink,
Mein Tic knock knock, mein Bom bom bom,
Mein Zoom zoom zoom, das ist mein Cymbal.

6 Johnny Schmoker, Johnny Schmoker,
Ich kann spielen, ich kann spielen,
Ich kann spiel mein kleine Viol.
Fal lal lal, das ist mein Viol,
Zoom zoom zoom, das ist mein Cymbal,
Bom bom bom, das ist mein Trombone,
Tic knock knock, das ist Triangle,
Pilly willy wink, das ist mein Fifie,
Rub a dub a dub, das ist mein Drummel.
Mein Rub a dub a dub, mein Pilly willy wink,
Mein Tic knock knock, mein Bom bom bom,
Mein Zoom zoom zoom, mein Fal lal lal,
Das ist mein Viol.

7. Johnny Schmoker, Johnny Schmoker,
Ich kann spielen, ich kann spielen,
Ich kann spiel mein kleine Toodle-Sach.
Whack whack whack, das ist mein Toodle-Sach,
Fal lal lal, das ist mein Viol,
Zoom zoom zoom, das ist mein Cymbal,
Bom bom bom, das ist mein Trombone,
Tic knock knock, das ist Triangle,
Pilly willy wink, das ist mein Fifie,
Rub a dub a dub, das ist mein Drummel.
Mein Rub a dub a dub, mein Pilly willy wink,
Mein Tic knock knock, mein Bom bom bom,
Mein Zoom zoom zoom, mein Fal lal lal,
Mein Whack whack whack,
Das ist mein Toodle-Sach.

SOLDIER'S FAREWELL.

KINKEL.

Andante.
poco riten
1st & 2nd Tenor.
1. How can I bear to leave thee, One part - ing kiss I give thee; And
2. Ne'er more may I be - hold thee, Or to this heart en - fold thee; With
3. I think of thee with long - ing, Think then, when tears are throng-ing, What
1st & 2nd Bass.
crescendo e poco accel.
a tempo.
then what e'er be - falls me, I go where hon - or calls me. Fare-
spear and pen - non glanc - ing, I see the foe ad - vanc - ing, Fare-
with my last faint sigh - ing, I'll whis - per soft while dy - ing, Fare-
cresc.
tranquillo e molto express.
well, fare well, my own true love, Fare - well, fare - well, my own true love.

HERE'S TO THE MAIDEN.

Allegro moderato.
From the "School for Scandal."
Voice.
Piano.
1. Here's to the maid-en of bash-ful fif-teen, Here's to the wi-dow of fif - - ty;
2. Here's to the charmer whose dimples we prize, Now to the maid who has none, sir;
3. Here's to the maid with a bo-som of snow, Now to her that's as brown as a ber - - ry;
Here's to the flaunting ex-trav-a-gant quean, And here's to the house-wife that's thrif - ty.
Here's to the girl with a pair of blue eyes, And here's to the nymph with but one, sir.
Here's to the wife with a face full of woe, And here's to the dam-sel that's mer - ry.
Let the toast pass, drink to the lass;— I war-rant she'll prove an excuse for the glass.
CHORUS.
ff Let the toast pass, drink to the lass;— I war-rant she'll prove an ex-cuse for the glass.
brillante.

REVELRY OF THE DYING.

Written by a British officer in India, at a time when the plague was hourly sweeping off his companions. He did not long survive his wonderful production.

Air.—"AWAY WITH MELANCHOLY"

1. We meet 'neath the sound - ing raf - ter, And the walls a - round are
bare, As they shout to our peals of laugh - ter, It seems that the dead are there.
But stand to your glasses, stea - dy! We drink to our comrades' eyes, Quaff a
cup to the dead al - rea - - dy, And hur - rah! for the next that dies.

2. Not a sigh for the lot that darkles;
Not a tear for the friends that sink;
We'll fall 'midst the wine-cup's sparkles,
As mute as the wine we drink.
So stand to your glasses, steady!
'Tis this that respite buys;
One cup to the dead already;
Hurrah! for the next that dies.

3. There's a mist on the glass congealing;
'Tis the hurricane's fiery breath
And thus does the warmth of feeling
Turn ice in the grasp of death.
Ho! stand to your glasses, steady!
For a moment the vapour flies;
A cup to the dead already;
Hurrah! for the next that dies.

4. Who dreads to the dust returning?
Who shrinks from the sable shore?
Where the high and haughty yearning
Of the soul shall sting no more.
Ho! stand to your glasses, steady!
The world is a world of lies;
A cup to the dead already;
Hurrah! for the next that dies.

5. Cut off from the land that bore us,
Betrayed by the land we find,
Where the brightest have gone before us,
And the dullest remain behind.
Stand! stand to your glasses, steady!
'Tis all we have left to prize;
A cup to the dead already,
And hurrah! for the next that dies.

AWAY, AWAY, AWAY!
Words by B. MORTON JONES '91.
Adapted from DE BERIOT.
Allegretto.
1. Air - i - ly float we with gen - tle swing, Out o'er the waters our voi - ces ring;
2. Out o'er the waters with dip - ping blade, By thoughts of the mor - row un - dis - mayed,
2. Ripples of laughter our plea - sure tell, 'Tis sweeter than rambling by wood and dell,
Joy-ful - ly, sweet - ly, we sing, we sing, A - way! a - way! a - - way!
Sorrow and sad - ness a - side are laid, A - way! a - way! a - - way!
Gaily to ride o'er the heav - ing swell, A - way! a - way! a - - way!
dim.
animato.
rit. e dim.
a tempo.
A - way, a - way, o'er the wa - ters clear, A - way, a - way, a - way! Where the
moon - light streams in ra - diant beams, Glim - mer - ing far and near,..........
and near.
AURA LEE.
Dolce.
cresc.
VOICES
PIANO.
1. As the black-bird, in the spring, 'Neath the wil - low tree, Sat and piped, I
2. On her cheek the rose was born, And her soft blue eyes, Like the dew - y
3. Like a sun - lit rippling brook, Was her laughing voice, From her eyes one
cresc.

cresc.
CHORUS.
heard him sing, Sing-ing Au-ra Lee.......
flowers of morn, Shone with glad sur-prise.......
gold-en look Made the world re-joice.......
Au-ra Lee! Au-ra Lee!
cresc.
mf
cresc.
Maid of gold-en hair! Sunshine came a-long with thee, And swallows in the air.....
cresc.
p
FORSAKEN AM I.
1st & 2nd Tenor.
pp Slow.
KOSCHAT.
1. For-sak-en, for-sak-en, For-sak-en am I! Like a stone by the road-side, All
2. A mound's in that churchyard, Fair buds o'er it break, And there sleeps my dar-ling, And
Air
1st & 2nd Bass
men pass me by; I go to a graveyard, No hope my heart cheers. There sad-ly I
will not a-wake; Each day do I stay there, To weep by the stone, And bit-ter-ly
kneel me, And shed bit-ter tears, There sad-ly I kneel me, And shed bit-ter tears.
feel there That on earth I'm a-lone, And bit-ter-ly feel there That on earth I'm a-lone.

I'SE GWINE BACK TO DIXIE.

C. A. WHITE.

Allegretto. Not too fast.
Voice.
Piano.
1. I'se gwine back to Dix - ie No more I'se gwine to wan - der, My heart's turn'd back to Dix - ie, I can't stay here no long - er. I miss de ole plan - ta - tion, My home and my re - la - tion, My heart's turned back to Dix - ie, And I must go.
2. I've hoed in fields of cot - ton, I've worked up - on the riv - er, I used to think if I got off I'd go back there no nev - er. But time has changed the old man, His head is bend - ing low...... His heart's turned back to Dix - ie, And he must go.
3. I'm trav - 'ling back to Dix - ie,— My step is slow and fee - ble, I pray the Lord to help me, And lead me from all e - vil. And should my strength for - sake me, Then, kind friends come and take me, My heart's turned back to Dix - ie, And I must go.
ad lib
colla voce
CHORUS.
I'se gwine back to Dix - ie, I'se gwine back to Dix ie, I'se

gwine where the or - ange blos - soms grow. For I hear the chil - dren
calling, I see their sad tears falling. My heart's turn'd back to Dix - ie, And I must go.
ad lib.
Andantino espressivo.
P. GLUCK, 1814.
1. Far in a shad - ed val - - ley, A wa - ter - mill ap - pears; But
In ei - nem küh - len Grun - - de, Da geht ein Müh - len - - rad; Mein
she I love has van - ished From scenes of hap - pier years; But
Lieb - chen ist ver - - schwun - den Das dort ge - woh - net hat; Mein
she I love has van - - ished From scenes of hap - pier years.
Lieb - chen ist ver - schwun - - den. Das dort ge - woh - - net hat.

THE BROKEN RING.

2. She promised to be faithful,
She pledged it with a ring,
But faithless hath she proven,
Her gift in twain did spring.

3. How sadly now as minstrel
Throughout the world I'd roam,
My weary ballad singing,
Afar from friends and home.

4. As soldier would I hasten,
Where rages fierce the fight;
And by the watch-fire linger,
Through all the gloomy night.

5. Yet whilst the mill I'm hearing,
I know not what my mind;
Ah! would my days were ended,
I then should quiet find.

2. Sie hat mir Treu' versprochen,
Gab mir ein'n Ring dabei,
Sie hat die Treu' gebrochen,
Das Ringlein sprang entzwei.

3. Ich möcht' als Spielmann reisen
Weit in die Welt hinaus,
Und singen meine Weisen,
Und gehn von Haus zu Haus.

4. Ich möcht' als Reiter fliegen
Wohl in die blut'ge Schlacht,
Um stille Feuer liegen
Im Feld bei dunkler Nacht.

5. Hör' ich das Mühlrad gehen:
Ich weiss nicht, was ich will—
Ich möcht' am liebsten sterben,
Da wär's auf einmal still!

AUF WIEDERSEHN.

Translation by B. MORTON JONES, '91. MENDELSSOHN.

poco sostenuto
p
1. In ev' - ry land, by God's command, From dear - est friends we ev - - - er Must
1. Es ist bestimmt in Gott - es Rat, Dass man vom Liebsten, was man hat, Muss

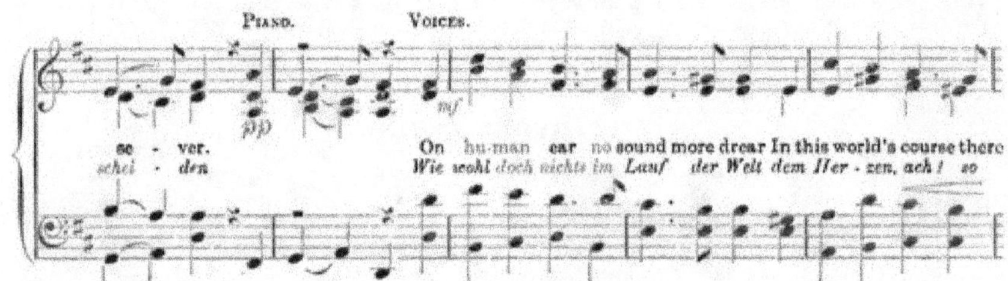
Piano.
Voices.
pp
mf
se - ver. On hu-man ear no sound more drear In this world's course there
schei - den Wie wohl doch nichts im Lauf der Welt dem Her - zen, ach! so

sf
Piano.
Voices.
e - ver fell, Than ah! fare-well, fare - well, fare - well.
sau - er fällt, als Schei - - den, ja Schei - - - den.

2. Should some loved friend a flower send,
A violet or rose-bud pure,
Of this be sure,—
Tho' in thy room at morn it bloom,
'Twill wither ere the night winds blow,
Yea! that I know.

3. Should Love's glad rays illume thy days,
And there be one to thee more fair
Than jewels rare:
She cannot stay with thee alway,
But far too quickly you must part,
With aching heart.

2. *So dir geschenkt ein Knösplein was,*
So thu'es in ein Wasserglas;
Doch wisse:
Blüht morgen dir ein Röslein auf,
Es welkt wohl schon die Nacht darauf,
Das wisse.

3. *Und hat dir Gott ein Lieb beschert,*
Und hältst du sie recht innig wert,
Die deine:
Es wird nur wenig Zeit wohl sein,
Da lässt sie dich so gar allein;
Dann weine!

Fourth verse only.
Piano.
Voices.
f
p
mf
4. When one must go and one remain, and one remain, When
4. Nun must du mich auch recht verstehn, ja recht verstehn. Wenn

whis - pers Hope "to meet a - gain," 'Tis then we say "Auf Wie - der - sehn, Auf
Men - chen aus - ein - an - der gehn, So sa - gen sie "Auf Wie - der - sehn, Auf
Piano. Voices.
Wie - der - sehn, Auf Wie - der - - sehn."

A HOME BY THE SEA.

Teneramente.

Words and Music by E. A. HOSMER.

Tenors
Air.
1. Oh! give me a home by the sea, Where wild waves are crest - ed with foam, Where shrill winds are car - ol - ing free, As
2. At morn, when the sun from the east Comes man - tled in crim - son and gold, Whose hues on the bil - lows are cast, Which
3. At eve, when the moon in her pride Rides queen of the soft summer night, And gleams on the mur - mur - ing tide, With

Basses

Piano.

o'er the blue waters they come, For I'd list to the ocean's loud
sparkles with splendour un - - - told. Oh! then by the shore would I
floods of her silver - y light. Oh! earth has no beau - ty so
roar, And joy in its stormiest glee, Nor ask in this wide world for
stray, And roam as the hal-cy-on free, From en - vy and care far a -
rare, No place that is dear-er to me. Then give me so free and so
more..................... Than a home by the deep heav - ing sea.
way..................... At my home by the deep heav - ing sea.
fair,..................... A home by the deep heav - ing sea.

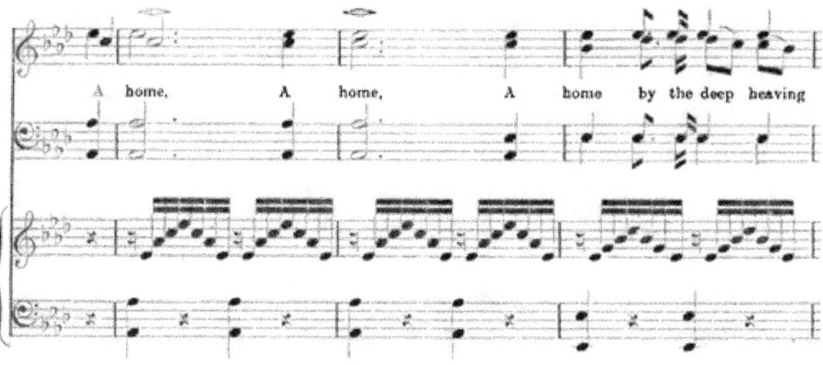

A home, A home, A home by the deep heaving

sea. A home, A home, A home by the deep heaving sea.

I'VE LOST MY DOGGY.

Con dolore.
Tenors
Basses
I've lost my dog - gy. Who's seen my bow - wow?
1st
2nd
Poor lit - tle dog - gy! Bow-wow-wow - wow! Bow-wow-wow - wow!

SLEIGH-RIDER'S SERENADE.

Words and Music by R. S. TAYLOR.

Tenors
1. The king of the north has clothed the earth In a robe of spot - less white; Ere
long the moon will mark the noon Of the ra - diant win - ter night. And
Basses
Piano.
under thy window, a-wait - ing there, Are steed and sleigh for thee, Then come away my
la - dy fair, A - way, a-way with me. O let us a-way, a - way, a-way, O
Ped.

let us a-way, away, away, O let us away, away, away, Where silv'ry moonbeams play.
Ped.
Ped.

2. A thousand eyes from out the skies
Will give us greeting kind;
With diamonds bright to reflect their light,
Our pathway shall be lined.
As swift as the course of a bird in air,
Our flight, our flight shall be;
Then come away, my lady fair,
Away, away with me.
Chorus.—O let us away, etc.

3. Night's goddess now about her brow
A misty halo wears;
A token to show that soon the snow
Will melt in rainy tears.
Ere ever the clouds shall gather there,
Or shining hours shall flee,
O haste away, my lady fair,
Away, away with me.
Chorus.—O let us away, etc.

EULALIE.

R. S. TAYLOR.

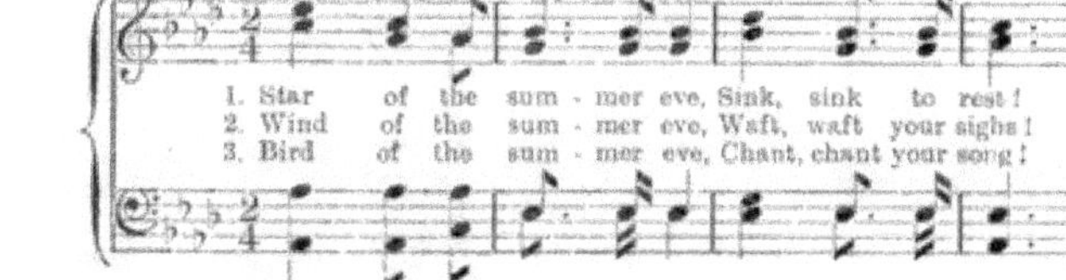
1. Star of the sum - mer eve, Sink, sink to rest! Sink ere the
2. Wind of the sum - mer eve, Waft, waft your sighs! From where the
3. Bird of the sum - mer eve, Chant, chant your song! While through the

sil - ver light Fades from the west; But ne - ver more will I
dis - tant hills Kiss gold - en skies; But ne - ver more will I
twi - light gleams Night's star - ry throng; But ne - ver more will I

Watch keep for thee, With her I lov'd so well, Sweet Eu - la - lie.
Wait here for thee, With her I lov'd so well, Sweet Eu - la - lie.
List here for thee, With her I lov'd so well, Sweet Eu - la - lie.

FAREWELL TO THE FOREST.

Andante non lento.
Arranged for Male voices from MENDELSSOHN.
p
f
1. O hills, O vales of plea - sure, O woods with verdure dressed, Where all the charms of
2. In sha - dy glen re - clin - ing, I trace the wrong and right; The beam of rea - son
3. And I must soon re - sign ye, For scenes of toil and strife; Ah! why does fate con-
p
When far from you I
The book I read is
Though called from you by
p
lei - sure, So oft have calmed my breast, When far from you I wan - - der,
shin - ing, Shows vir - tue ev - er bright— The book I read is Na - ture's,
sign me To play the farce of life? Though called from you by du - - - ty,
When far from you I wander,
The book I read is Nature's,
Though call'd from you by du - ty
f
pp
Lost in the worldly train, My heart will fond - ly pon - - der, And sigh for you a
There sim-ple truths ap - pear, And though she change her fea - - tures, Her dic - tates still are
Still, whereso - e'er I stray, The spir - it of your beau - - ty Will nev - er fade a-
pp
pon - - - - der, My
fea - - - - - tures, And
beau - - - - ty, The
dim.
f
p
gain, My heart will fond - ly pon - der, And sigh for you a - gain.
clear, And though she change her fea - tures, Her dic - tates still are clear.
way, The spir - it of your beau - ty Will ne - - ver fade a - way.
cresc.
heart will fond - ly pon - - - - - - der, (1st Bass) sigh .... for you a - gain.
though she change her fea - - - - - - tures, dic - - - - - - - tates still are clear.
spir it of your beau - - - - ty ne - - - - - - - ver fade a - way.

SPEED AWAY!

Among the superstitions of the Senecas is one which for its singular beauty is somewhat well known. When a maiden dies, they imprison a young bird until it first begins to try its powers of song, and then, loading it with kisses and caresses, they loose its bonds over her grave, in the belief that it will not fold its wings nor close its eyes, until it has flown to the spirit-land, and delivered its precious burden of affection to the loved and lost. "It is not unfrequent," says the Indian historian, "to see twenty or thirty birds set loose at once over one grave."

I. B. WOODBURY.

1. Speed a - way! speed a - way! on thine er - rand of light! There's a
2. Wilt thou tell her, bright song - ster, the old chief is lone? That he
young heart a - wait - ing thy com - ing to - night; She will fon - dle thee
sits all the day by his cheerless hearth-stone? That his tom - a - hawk
close, she will ask for the loved Who pine up - on earth since the
lies all un - not - ed the while, And his thin lips wreathe e - ver in-
"Day Star" has roved, She will ask if we miss her, so long is her
one sun - less smile? That the old chief - tian mourns her, and why will she
stay. Speed a - way! Speed a - way! Speed a - way!
stay? Speed a - way! Speed a - way! Speed a - way!
ritard.
dim.
DAL SEG.

3. And oh! wilt thou tell her, blest bird on the wing,
That her mother hath ever a sad song to sing?
That she standeth alone in the still quiet night,
And her fond heart goes forth for the being of night
Who had slept in her bosom, but who would not stay?
Speed away! speed away! speed away!

4. *Go, bird of the silver wing! fetterless now;
Stoop not thy bright pinions on yon mountain's brow,
But hie thee away o'er rock, river and glen,
And find our young "Day Star" ere night close again.
Up! onward! let nothing thy mission delay.
Speed away! speed away! speed away!

* *Accel.*

THE TEMPERANCE CORPS.
MARCHING SONG.
Quick March.
Brilliante.
Words and Music by F. SIMS.
PIANO.
SOLO. (Baritone.)
(Chorus) "You bet."
1. We're the "Temp'rance Corps" of the "Q. O. R.," and we ne'er get on the spree! We
ne - ver yet im - bibed a "wet" strong - er than "Li-Quor tea."
ten.
"You bet!"
CHORUS.
TENORS.
Then brace up! brace up!
BASSES.
Then brace up! brace up! brace up! brace up!
PIANO.

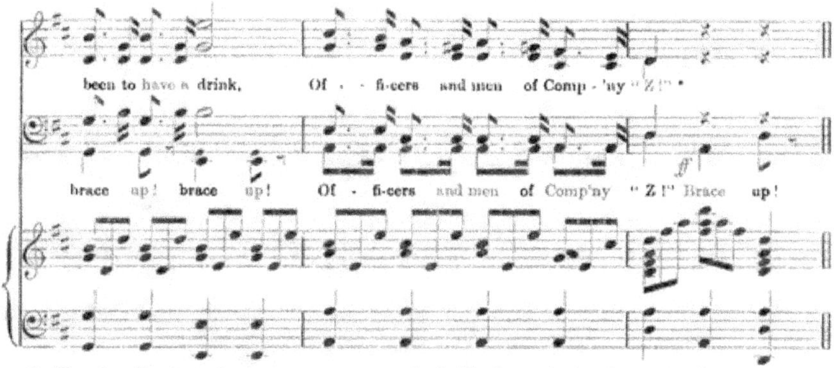

Vol - unteers should e - - ver so - ber be, Don't let the people think You've

brace up! brace up! brace up, brace up! brace up! brace up!

been to have a drink, Of - - fi-cers and men of Comp - 'ny "Z!" *

brace up! brace up! Of - fi-cers and men of Comp'ny "Z!" Brace up!

2. Though we'd not run from any gun,
We "pocket pistols" fear, (*Chorus*, "You bet")
We ne'er regale on "Ginger ale,"
"Rye splits" or "Lager bier." ("You bet.")
Chorus.—Then brace up, &c.

3. On "Drink Parade," "cool lemonade,"
We always meekly say, ("That's so.")
And no excuse could us induce
To "down a T. and J." ("Oh! no.")
Chorus.—Then brace up, &c.

4. We always shoot each raw recruit
Who dares to dream of beer, ("You bet.")
And by this plan make every man
A "model" volunteer. ("You bet.")
Chorus.—Then brace up, &c.

5. When we march out, the people shout
"Here comes the 'Temp'rance Corps,'" ("You bet.")
With three times three for Company "Z,"
† And the gallant Q.O.R. ("You bet.")
Chorus.—Then brace up, &c.

* Z pronounced *zee*. B, C, D, E, G, &c., may be used *ad lib.*

† *Or* Hip, hip, hurrah! hurrah!

THE STILL NIGHT.—A Catch.

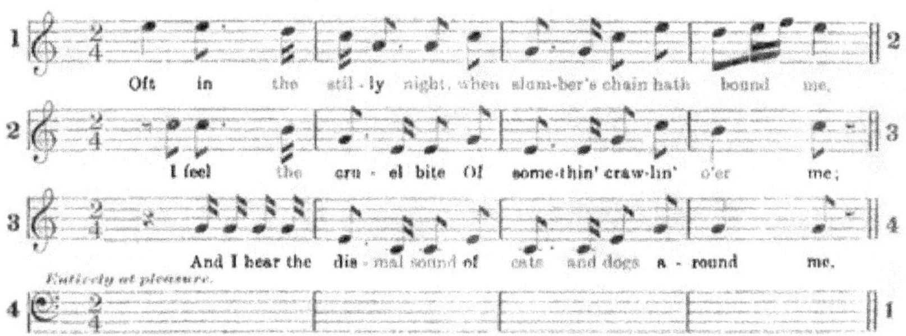
1
Oft in the stil - ly night, when slum-ber's chain hath bound me,
2
2
I feel the cru - el bite Of some-thin' craw-lin' o'er me;
3
3
And I hear the dis - mal sound of cats and dogs a - round me.
4
Entirely at pleasure.
4
Bow wow wow! phit phit! meow! phit phit! bow wow! meow meow! phit phit! bow wow! meow!
1

TREUE LIEBE.

Translation by J. D. SPENCE, '89.

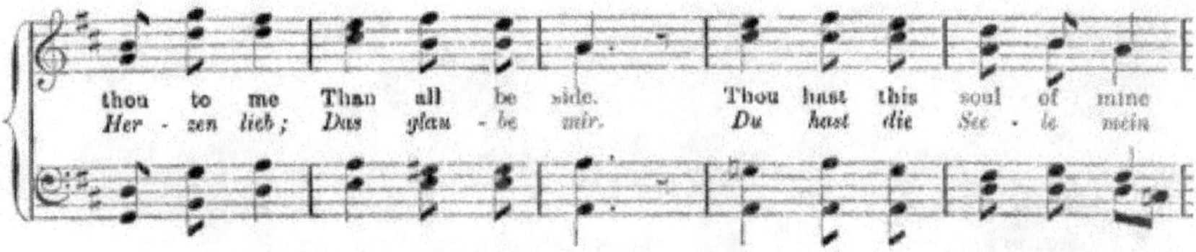

TENORS

BASSES

1. Ah! can it tru - ly be, That I must part from thee? Dear - er art thou to me Than all be side. Thou hast this soul of mine So close - ly knit to thine, I know no o - ther love Than thine a - lone.

1. Ach! wie ist's mög-lich dann, Dass ich dich las - sen kann? Hab' dich von Her - zen lieb; Das glau - be mir. Du hast die See - le mein So ganz ge - nom - men ein, Dass ich kein' and 're lieb, als dich all - ein.

2. Blue the forget-me-not,
Emblem of constancy;
Close press it to thy breast,
And think of me.
Though flower and hope decay,
Rich we in love alway:
My heart's deep love for thee
Never can die.

3. Were I a bird, on high
Far through the air I'd fly;
No hawk should daunt me then,
Winging to thee.
Struck by the huntsman's dart,
Sinking upon thy heart,
There, should'st thou weep for me,
Fain would I die.

2. *Blau ist ein Blümelein*
Das heisst Vergissnichtmein:
Dies Blümlein leg' ans Herz,
Und denke mein.
Stirbt Blum' und Hoffnung gleich,
Wir sind an Liebe reich,
Denn die stirbt nie bei mir;
Das glaube mir.

3. *Wär' ich ein Vögelein,*
Bald wollt' ich bei dir sein,
Scheut' Falk' und Habicht nicht,
Flög' schnell zu dir.
Schöss' mich ein Jäger tot,
Fiel ich in deinen Schoss,
Sah'st du mich traurig an,
Gern stürb' ich dann.

YE SHEPHERDS TELL ME.

MAZZINGHI.

Larghetto.
VOICE.
1. Ye shep - herds tell me, tell me have you seen,
2. A wreath a - round her head, a-round her head she wore, Car-
PIANO.
p

have you seen my Flo - ra pass this way, In shape and feature
na - - - - tion, Li - ly, Li - - - ly, Rose, And in her hand a
dolce
beau - ty's Queen. In pastoral, in pastoral ar - ray.
crook she bore, And sweets, and sweets her breath com-pose.
CHORUS.
f
have you
Shep-herds tell me, tell me, tell me have you seen, tell me have you
dolce.
have you
Have you seen, tell me
seen My Flo - ra pass this way; Shep - - herds,
seen, have you seen Have you seen, tell me
f dolce. rall.
Shepherds have you seen, tell me have you seen My Flo - ra pass this way?

Bass Voice.
The beau - - teous, the beau - teous wreath that decks her head,
Forms her des - crip - - tion, her des-crip - tion true.
Hands li - ly white. Lips crim-son red,
And cheeks, and cheeks of ro - sy hue.
Repeat Chorus

STARS OF THE SUMMER NIGHT.

Words by LONGFELLOW. J. D. KERRISON.

p
1. Stars of the sum - mer night, Far in yon a - zure deeps, Hide, hide your
p
gold - en light; She sleeps, my la - dy sleeps; .... She sleeps, my la - dy sleeps.

2. Moon of the summer night,
 Far down your western steeps,
Sink, sink in silver light;
 She sleeps, my lady sleeps.

3. Wind of the summer night,
 Where yonder woodbine creeps
Fold, fold your pinions light;
 She sleeps, my lady sleeps.

4. Dreams of the summer night,
 Tell her her lover keeps
Watch, while in slumber light
 She sleeps, my lady sleeps.

STARS OF THE SUMMER NIGHT.

1st & 2nd Tenor.
As sung at YALE.
1. Stars of the sum - mer night, Far in yon a - zure deeps,
1st & 2nd Bass.
Hide, hide your gold - en light; She sleeps, my la - - dy sleeps,
rall.
pp
She........................ sleeps, she sleeps, my la - - dy sleeps.

EN ROULANT MA BOULE.

1st time Solo.
FINE.
1. En rou - lant ma bou - le rou - lant, En rou - lant ma bou - le.
1st time Solo.
Der - rièr' chez nous ya t'un é - tang. En rou - lant ma bou - le.

Trois beaux can-ards s'en vont baig-nant, rou - li, rou-lant, ma bou - le rou - lant.
CHORUS. (Humming.)
1st and 2nd Tenors.
Hon hon, hon, hon, hon, hon, hon, hon, hon, hon, hon.
1st and 2nd Basses.

2. Trois beaux canards s'en vont baignant,
   En roulant ma boule.
Le fils du roi s'en va chassant,
Rouli, roulant, ma boule roulant.—*Ref.*

3. Le fils du roi s'en va chassant,
   En roulant ma boule,
Avec son grand fusil d'argent,
Rouli, roulant, ma boule roulant.—*Ref.*

4. Avec son grand fusil d'argent.
   En roulant ma boule,
Visa le noir, tua le blanc,
Rouli, roulant, ma boule roulant.—*Ref.*

5. Visa le noir, tua le blanc.
   En roulant ma boule,
O fils du roi, tu es méchant!
Rouli, roulant, ma boule roulant.—*Ref.*

6. O fils du roi, tu es méchant!
   En roulant ma boule,
D'avoir tué mon canard blanc,
Rouli, roulant, ma boule roulant.—*Ref.*

7. D'avoir tué mon canard blanc,
   En roulant ma boule,
Par dessous l'aile il perd son sang,
Rouli, roulant, ma boule roulant.—*Ref.*

8. Par dessous l'aile il perd son sang,
   En roulant ma boule,
Par les yeux lui sort'nt des diamants,
Rouli, roulant, ma boule roulant.—*Ref.*

9. Par les yeux lui sort'nt des diamants,
   En roulant ma boule,
Et par le bec l'or et l'argent,
Rouli, roulant, ma boule roulant.—*Ref.*

10. Et par le bec l'or et l'argent,
   En roulant ma boule,
Toutes ses plum's s'en vont au vent
Rouli, roulant, ma boule roulant.—*Ref.*

11. Toutes ses plum's s'en vont au vent,
   En roulant ma boule,
Trois dam's s'en vont les ramassant,
Rouli, roulant, ma boule roulant.—*Ref.*

12. Trois dam's s'en vont les ramassant,
   En roulant ma boule,
C'est pour en faire un lit de camp,
Rouli, roulant, ma boule roulant.—*Ref.*

13 C'est pour en faire un lit de camp,
   En roulant ma boule,
Pour y coucher tous les passants,
Rouli, roulant, ma boule roulant.—*Ref.*

BRIDGET DONAHUE.

Music by A. S. JOSSELYN.

VOICE.
PIANO.
1. It was in the Coun-ty Ker-ry, A lit-tle way from Clare, Where the boys and girls are mer-ry at a pat-ron race or fair; The town is called Kel-lor-glin, a pur-ty place to view, But what makes it in-ter-est-ing is my Brid-get Don-a-hue!
CHORUS: Oh Brid-get Don-a-hue, I real-ly do love you, Al-though I'm in A-mer-i-ca, to you I will be true; Then Brid-get Don-a-hue, I'll tell you what I'll do, Just take the name of Pat-ter-son and I'll take Don-a-hue!
Repeat for Chorus.

2. Her father is a farmer, and a decent man is he,
He's liked by all the people from Kellorglin to Tralee;
And Bridget on a Sunday, when coming home from mass,
She's admired by all the people, sure they wait to see her pass.

3. I sent her home a picture, I did upon my word,
Not a picture of myself, but the picture of a bird:
It was the American Eagle, and says I, "Miss Donahue,
Our eagle's wings are large enough to shelter me and you!"

HALLI-HALLO.

Words by WILHELM BORNEMANN, 1816. Translation by J. EDMUND JONES, '88.

BARITONE SOLO
VOICE.
PIANO.
1. Through wood and fo - rest rang - ing, I find a joy un - chang - - ing, A
1. Im Wald und auf der Hai - de, Da such' ich mei - ne Freu - - de Ich
2. My dog is good and trus - ty, Our ap - pe-tites are lus - - ty: A
2. Zur Er - de hin - ge - streck - et, Den Tisch mit Moos mir deck - - et Die
hunts - man bold am I......... A hunts - man bold am I.........
bin ein Jä - gers - mann,..... Ich bin ein Jä - gers - - mann.....
meal I soon pre - pare,....... A meal I soon pre - pare......
freund - li - che Na - tur;...... Die freund - li - - che Na - tur;......
My heart is e'er de - light - - ed, To see the deer, af - fright - - ed, From
Den Wald und Forst zu he - - gen, Das Wild - pret zu er - le - - gen Mein'
Up - on the ground re - clin - - ing, From mos - sy ta - ble din - - ing, We
Den treu - en Hund zur Sei - - te, Ich mir das Mahl be - rei - - te Auf
CHORUS.
out his co - - vert fly,............ From out his co - vert fly.......
Lust hab' ich dar - an............ Mein' Lust hab' ich dar - an........
eat our fru - - gal fare........... We eat our fru - gal fare......
Got - tes frei - - er Flur.......... Auf Got - - tes frei - er Flur.......

Whistle.
Warble.
Tenors.
Hal - - li, hal-lo, hal - li, hal-lo,
From out his co - - vert fly..........
Mein' Lust hab' ich dar-an.........
We eat our fru - - gal fare........
Auf Got - tes frei - - er Flur.........
Hal -
Air. Basses.

li, hal-lo, hal - li, hal-lo,
From out his co - vert fly.........
Mein' Lust hab' ich dar - an.........
We eat our fru - - gal fare........
Auf Got - tes frei - - er Flur.......

3. I, though without a nickel,
My dainty palate tickle
With wine and good black bread.
My fragrant pipe burns brightly,
As, stepping forward lightly,
The flow'ry heath I tread.

4. Thus, in the fields abiding,
Or through the forest striding,
I pass the livelong day,
And while my hours are fleeting
Like seconds swift retreating,
I through the green-wood stray.

5. And now the sun is sinking,
Now stars through mists are blinking;
Thus one more day slips by;
So home again returning,
Where cheerful hearth is burning,
A jolly huntsman I.

3. *Kein Heller in der Tasche,*
Ein Schlücklein in der Flasche,
Ein Stückchen schwarzes Brod;
Brennt lustig meine Pfeife,
Wenn ich den Forst durchstreife,
Da hat es keine Noth.

4. *So zieh' ich durch die Walder,*
So eil' ich durch die Felder,
Wohl hin den ganzen Tag;
Dann fliehen meine Stunden
Gleich flüchtigen Sekunden,
Tracht' ich dem Wilde nach.

5. *Wenn sich die Sonne neiget,*
Der feuchte Nebel steiget,
Mein Tagwerk ist gethan.
Dann zieh' ich von der Haide
Zur häuslichstillen Freude,
Ein froher Jägersmann.

ON THE BANKS OF THE YANG-TSEE-KIANG.

Words by REV. J. DAVISON. Adapted by J. L. MORRISON.

Voice. Solo

Piano.

1. My name is Polly Hill, and I had a lover Bill, Whose fate cost me many a
2. Oh! the war it soon broke out, I don't know what 'twas 'bout, But let those that make war go

Chorus. Solo. Chorus.

pang, pang, For his reg'ment took the rout, and he went to the right about, To the banks of the Yang-Yang-
bang, bang, So he went with thousands ten to fight the Chinamen, On the banks of the Yang-Yang-

Yang-t-see-ki-ang, To the banks of the Yang-t-see-ki-ang.
Yang-t-see-ki-ang, On the banks of the Yang-t-see-ki-ang.

3. Three years had passed away, whilst it fell upon a day,
That I sat by my door and span, span,
That a soldier came and said, "Your lover Bill lies dead
On the banks of the Yang-Yang-Yang-tsee-kiang,
On the banks of the Yang-tsee-kiang.

4. "'Twas in a tea-tree glen that we met the Chinamen,
And one of the rogues let bang, bang,
Which laid poor William low, with his toes towards the foe,
On the banks of the Yang-Yang-Yang-tsee-kiang,
On the banks of the Yang-tsee-kiang.

5. "He took a sprig of tea and said, 'Will you carry this for me,
And tell poor Polly where it sprang, sprang?'
And this was all he said, when his head it dropped like lead,
On the banks of the Yang-Yang-Yang-tsee-kiang,
On the banks of the Yang-tsee-kiang.

6. "Now will you take from me this little sprig of tea?
'Twas on Bill's grave that it sprang, sprang,
You may have it if you will, as a souvenir of Bill,
From the banks of the Yang-Yang-Yang-tsee-kiang,
From the banks of the Yang-tsee-kiang."

7. "My soldier boy," said I, "do you see any green in my eye?
Pray excuse me the use of slang, slang,
For I'm your Polly Hill, and you're my lover Bill,
From the banks of the Yang-Yang-Yang-tsee-kiang,
From the banks of the Yang-tsee-kiang."

THE CLOUD CAP'T TOWERS.

SHAKESPEARE, "The Tempest," Act IV., s. I. R. I. STEVENS.

1st & 2nd Alto
mf
The cloud cap't tow - ers, the gor - geous pa - la - ces, the
f
p
Slow.
1st & 2nd Tenors 8ve lower
the gor - geous pa - la - ces, the
Slow. mf
1st & 2nd Bass
the
Slow.
Piano
mf

so - - lemn tem - ples, the great globe it - self, yea, all which it in -
so - - lemn tem - ples, the great globe it - self, yea, all which it in -
so - - lemn tem - ples, the great globe it - self, yea, all which it in -
f

pp
cresc
p
- - he - rit, shall dis - - solve,.. and, like the base-less fa - bric of a
pp
cresc.
p
- - he - rit, shall dis - - solve,.. and, like the base-less fa - bric of a
pp
cresc.
p
- - he - rit, shall dis - - solve,.. and, like the base-less fa - bric of a
pp
p

pp
pp
vi - - sion, leave not a wreck be - hind, leave not a wreck be - hind.
pp
vi - - sion, leave not a wreck be - hind.
pp
vi - - sion, leave not a wreck be - hind.
pp
pp

KERMESSE SCENE.*

FROM "FAUST."

GOUNOD.

Allegretto.
Voices.
Piano.
Red or white li - quor, Coarse or fine! What can it matter, So we have
wine? What if the vin - tage Great be or small? Your jol-ly to - per drink-eth of
all.
Solo. (Wagner.)
Stu - dent vers'd in ev - 'ry bar - rel, Save the one of wa-ter
white, To thy glo - ry, to thy love, Drink a - way... to -
stacc.

* By permission of Messrs. Chappell & Co., London, Eng.

1st Basses.
night! Stu - dent vers'd in ev - 'ry bar - rel, Save the one of water
white, To thy glo - - ry, to thy love, Drink a - - way........ to-
cres cen - do. f
night....
p

2ND BASSES. (Soldiers.)
Young girls, an - - - cient cas - tles, They are
cres - cen - do.
all the same; Old towns, dain - - - ty maidens, are a -
like our game; For the he - ro,.........., brave and tender, Makes of
ff
both his prey: Both to va-lour........ must sur-ren-der, And a ran-som
f

pay! And a ran-som pay!............
1st Tenors. (Old men.)
Each new Sun-day
pp
brings the old sto-ry, Dan-ger gone by, How we enjoy! While, to-day each
hot-headed boy Fights for to-day's lit-tle glo - - - ry! Let me but sit,

co - sy and dry, un - der the trees with my daugh - - ter, And while raft and
boat travel by, Drink to the folk on the wa - - ter! Let me but sit
co - sy and dry, Un - der the trees with my daugh - - ter, And while raft and
DA CAPO AL ⊕ THEN TO FINE
FINE
boat travel by, Drink to the folk on the wa - - ter! night.....
8va. FINE.
DA CAPO AL ⊕ THEN TO FINE.

SLEEP, LADY, SLEEP!

SERENADE.

Largo. H. R. BISHOP, 1780-1855.

TENORS / BASSES

pp

Sleep, la - dy, sleep!... The sum - mer night doth fall, With sil-ver moon-light soft - - ly stream - - - - - ing;.... The night breeze sighs through all the hap - py hours, Be - neath thy case-ment droop the drow - sy flow'rs.

stream - - ing o'er all;..

express. *pp*

dolce

droop the drow - sy flow'rs.

Allegretto moderato

p

Sleep, and may dreams of sweet de - - - light vi - - sit thee, love, this sum - - mer night.

p

Sleep, la - dy, sleep! and may no sor - - row Come nigh thee e - - ver on a - - ny

cresc. *dim.*

mor - row, Come nigh thee, lov'd one, ev - - - - - er.
Come .... nigh thee ev - - - - - - er.
pp
Sleep, and may dreams of sweet de - - - light vi - sit thee,
love, this sum - mer night.................. Good night......
Good night, good
night. Good night, good
night.
.... good night, good night, good night. Sleep on with dreams of
cresc. f
sweet de - light. Good night, good night, good night, good
dim.
night, good night, good night................
ppp

JUANITA.

SPANISH BALLAD.

HON. MRS. NORTON.

Allegretto.
p
1. Soft o'er the foun - tain, Ling-'ring falls the southern moon;
2. When, in thy dream - ing, Moons like these shall shine a - gain,
Far o'er the moun - tain, Breaks the day too soon! In thy dark eyes'
And day-light beam - ing Prove thy dreams are vain— Wilt thou not, re-
splen - dor, Where the warm light loves to dwell,.... Wea - ry looks, yet ten - - der,
lent - ing, For thine ab - sent lov - er sigh,.... In thy heart con-sent - - ing
Slower
a tempo.
Ni - ta! *Jua - ni - ta!
Speak their fond fare - well! Ni - ta! Ni - ta! Ask thy soul if
To a prayer gone by? Ni - ta! Ni - ta! Let me ling - er
mf
Ni - ta! Jua - - - ni ta!
Tenderly
slow
we should part! Ni - ta! Ni - ta! Lean thou on my heart.
by thy side! Ni - ta! Ni - ta! Be my own fair bride!

* Pronounced "Waneeta."

GLORY AND LOVE TO THE MEN OF OLD.*

THE CELEBRATED CHORUS OF SOLDIERS IN "FAUST."

Tempo marziale. GOUNOD.

Tenors
Basses
Piano.
Glo - - ry and love to the men of old,...... Their sons may
co-py their vir - tues bold;.... Cour - - age in heart and a sword in hand,....
Ready to fight or ready to die for Fa - - - ther - land! Who needs bidding to dare ...

* By permission of Messrs. Chappell & Co., London, Eng.

...... by a trumpet blown? Who lacks pity to spare.......... when the field is won?....
Who would fly from a foe.................. if a-lone, or last?...... And
boast he was true, as coward might do when pe - - - ril is past?

cresc.
Glo - - - ry and love to the men of old!........ Their sons may
cresc.
molto. cresc.
copy their vir-tues bold,....... Cour - - age in heart and a sword in hand,....
molto. cresc.
ff
Ready to fight for Fa - - - - - ther-land....... Now............ to home a-
ff
ff

gain,............ we come, the long and fie-ry strife of bat - tle o - - ver,......
Rest.............. is pleas-ant af - - - - - - ter toil as hard as ours be-neath a stranger
Rest .... is pleasant af - - - - - - ter toil be - neath.............. a stranger
sun. .. Many.... a maid-en fair.............. is waiting
sun, beneath a wild and stranger sun.............. The maiden fair.............. is waiting

here to greet her truant sol-dier lov - er,......... And many a heart............ will fail and
will fail........ and
brow............ grow pale to hear............... to hear the tale of cru - el pe - ril he has
brow grow pale...... to hear, to hear.. the tale of cru - el pe - ril he has
dim.
cresc.
run,...................... And many a heart. .... and many a
run, And many............ a heart, And heart will fail, and many a
cre - - - - - scen - - - -
p

dim.
p
heart will fail and brow grow pale to hear the tale of pe - ril he has run.
dim.
crescendo.
f
f
ff
Glo - - - - ry and love to the men of old!.... Their sons may
ff
ff
copy their vir-tues bold;.... Cour - - age in heart and a sword in hand,..

Ready to fight for Fa - - ther-land,
or ready to die
for Fa - - ther-
or ready to fight
land,
or ready to die,............
or ready to die..................
for
or ready to fight
rit.
Fa - - - ther - land,..................
rit. p
f
ff

SAILING ACROSS THE SEA.

Words by H. L. D'ARCY JAXONE.
VERNON REY.
VOICE.
PIANO.
Andante grazioso.
f
dim.
rit.
p
1. On a
2. On a
3. O'er the
paint - ed o - cean a paint - - ed ship Is hung on the home - stead
paint - ed o - cean a paint - - ed ship Is hid in the dark - en'd
sum - mer o - cean a white wing'd ship Is float - ing across the
wall; To the mo - ther's eyes, and the mo - ther's heart, The
room; For a sha - - dow stole from a sou - thern sea, And
foam; And the cast - - a - - way that they found at sea Is
ho - li - est thing of all............ For a lad with a tan - gle of
shroud - ed the house in gloom... So they hid from the mo - ther the
al - most in sight of home.......... Then a head with a tan - gle of
legato
mf

cresc.
molto cresc.
gol - den hair, The light of her eyes was he; In that gal - lant ves-sel a
miss - ing ship, And hop'd that the best might be; Ere they told the tale that all
gol - den hair Is bowed on a mo - ther's knee; And a mes - sage from heav'n to
molto cresc.
rall.
molto rall.
pp
year a - go, Went sail - ing across the sea................
hands were lost, While sail - ing across the sea................
earth to-day Comes sail - ing across the sea................
molto rall cresc.
CHORUS.
Andante grazioso.
1st & 2nd Tenor.
dim.
Air.
Sail - - - ing, Sail - - - ing, Sail - ing a - cross the sea....
1st & 2nd Bass.
Sail - ing, Sail - ing, Sail - ing, Sail - ing, Sail - ing a - cross the sea, a - cross the
Andante grazioso.

Lento.
Sail - - ing, sail - - ing, Sail - ing a - cross the sea...
Air.
sea.... Sail - ing, sail - ing, sail ing a - - - - cross the sea........
sf
lento

BREATHE SOFT, YE WINDS.

Andante affettuoso. WILLIAM PAXTON, 1781.

Breathe soft, ye winds, ye wa - ters gent - ly flow,..

Shield her ye trees, ye flow'rs a - round her grow; Ye swains, I

beg you, pass in si - lence by,.... My love.......... in yon - der vale

a - sleep doth lie, My love........ in yon - der vale a - sleep doth lie.

FAREWELL.

Volkslied, known in 1690.
Translation by F. J. DAVIDSON, '91. *Andante.* SILCHER, 1827.

VOICES. PIANO.

1. When the gol - den dawn of day Sends the sun - - beams dart - ing,
2. When two ge - nial souls are friends, Friendship ne - - ver pal - ters,
1. *Mor - gen muss ich fort von hier und muss Ab - - schied neh - men.*

Heart from heart must hence a - way, Torn by pangs.... of part - ing:
Be it joy or grief fate sends, Friendship ne - - ver al - ters.
O du al - ler - schön - ste Zier, Schei - den, das.... bringt Grä - men.

Why, oh why may I not stay? Fate should never so - - ver
How much keen - er is the pain, When with longing o'er the main,
Da ich dich so treu ge - liebt, ü - ber al - le Mas - sen,

Hearts that love for e - - - ver, Hearts that love for e - ver.
True love faints and fal - - - ters, True love faints and fal - ters.
soll ich dich ver - - las - - - sen, soll ich dich ver - las - sen.

3. Shall I then my whole life through
Leave my hopes behind me?
In strange lands so far from you
Joy can never find me.
If I've ever grieved you, sweet,
Pardon, I am at your feet,
Love and sorrow bind me.

2. *Wenn zwei gute Freunde sind,*
Die einander kennen—
Sonn' und Mond bewegen sich
Ehe sie sich trennen.
Wie viel grösser ist der Schmerz,
Wenn ein treu verliebtes Herz
In die Fremde ziehet!

3. *Dort auf jener grünen Au'*
Steht mein jung frisch Leben;
Soll ich denn mein Lebenlang
In der Fremde schweben!
Hab' ich dir was Leids gethan,
Bitt' dich woll's vergessen,
Denn es geht zu Ende.

4. Fancy it a sigh from me,
If the breeze but kiss you,
From across the sundering sea
Come to tell I miss you;
Hopes are past that were to be.
Still my soul is yearning—
Is there no returning?

4. *Küsset dir ein Lüftelein*
Wangen oder Hände;
Denke, dass es Seufzer sei'n,
Die ich zu dir sende.
Tausend schick' ich täglich aus,
Die da wehen um dein Haus,
Weil ich dein gedenke.

LE DRAPEAU DE CARILLON.

At Carillon (now Ticonderoga), on Lake Champlain, Montcalm in 1758 drove back the English forces under General Abercrombie. A French soldier, after a vain attempt to rouse his nation to a sense of the danger in which their possessions on this continent were placed, returns to the scene of his former victory, and is supposed there to give utterance to the words of the song.

Words by OCTAVE CRÉMAZIE.
Translation by B. MORTON JONES, '91.

CHARLES W. SABATIER.
Arr. by T. MARTENS.

Largement. Solo.
1. O Ca-ril-lon, je te revois enco - re, Non plus, hélas! comme en ces jours bénis,
1. O Ca-ril-lon, to thee once more returning, Sad - ly I gaze on thy famil - iar wall;
2. Mes compagnons, d'u - ne vaine es-péran - ce, Ber - çant en-cor leurs coeurs toujours français,
2. In vain my com-rades' cheeks are warmly glowing, In vain they lull with dreams of home their pain,
Piano.
Où, dans tes murs, la trompet-te son-o - re, Pour te sauver nous a - vait ré - u-nis.
Not as of yore, when hearts with ardor burning Throng'd thee to save at the loud bugle-call.
Les yeux tournés du cô - té de la Fran - ce, Di - ront souvent: Re-viend-ront— ils jamais?
In vain to France their heart is ev-er go - ing, Filled with this hope, "Will they come back again?"
CHORUS. Agitato.
Je viens.... à toi quand mon â - me...... suc-com - - be
To thee.... I come when low my heart.... is beat - - ing,
L'il - - lu - - si - on con - - so - le - ra...... leur vi - - e;
This hope,.. tho' vain, will be their con - - so - la - - tion,
Agitato.

Et sent.... dé-jà son.... cou-ra - ge fai - blir,
When cou - rage fails, and........ all a-round is drear,
Moi, sans.... es-poir, quand.. mes jours vont fi - ir,
But when at last my lone - ly death is near,
Oui, près.. de toi,.......... ve - nant cher - cher.... ma tom - - be,
Yea! near.. to thee.......... my death more brave - ly meet - ing,
Et sans.. at - tendre........ u - ne pa - role a - mi - - e,
Naught shall be mine........ of friend - ship's ad - mir - a - - tion,—
Pour mon.. dra-peau je viens.. i-ci.... mou-rir.........
Guard - ing my flag, I come.. to per - ish here,.......

3. *Cet étendard, qu'au grand jour des batailles,*
Noble Montcalm, tu plaças dans ma main,
Cet étendard qu'aux portes de Versailles,
Naguère, hélas! je déployais en vain,
Je te remets aux champs où de ta gloire
Vivra toujours l'immortel souvenir,
Et dans ma tombe emportant ta mémoire,
Pour mon drapeau je viens ici mourir.

4. *Qu'ils sont heureux ceux qui dans la mêlée*
Près de Lévis moururent en soldats!
En expirant, leur âme consolée,
Voyait la gloire adoucir leur trépas.
Vous qui dormez dans votre froide bière,
Vous que j'implore à mon dernier soupir,
Réveillez-vous! Apportant ma bannière,
Sur vos tombeaux, je viens ici mourir.

3. Noble Montcalm, thou gavest me this standard,
'Midst shot and shell upon the battle plain,
Bearing it, lately to Versailles I wandered,
But there, alas! I unfurled it in vain.
Back now I place it where the recollection
Of thy great deeds shall ne'er fade or grow sere,
And unto death shall last my deep affection,—
Guarding my flag I come to perish here.

4. Thrice happy they to whom by fate 'twas given
'Mid the brave throng near Levi's height to die,
For them the cloud by one glad ray was riven,
Glory could sweeten their sad destiny.
Ye who now slumber till the great awaking,
On whom I call with dying accents clear,—
Awake! my banner in my hand I'm taking,
Upon your graves I come to perish here.

DIGGY-DADDY, HEAR HIM WEEP.

SOLO.
Arr. by T. MARTENS.
VOICE.
PIANO.
1. Ole mas - sa bought a bran new coat, and hung it in the hall, The
2. Ole mas - sa bought a bran new girl, he got her in the Souf', Her
3. Oh! Ma - ry had a lit - tle corn up - on her lit - tle toe, And
dar - kies stole that coat a - way, and wore it to the ball.
hair it curled so ve - ry tight, she could - n't shut her mouf.
ev - 'ry - where that Ma - ry went, the corn was sure to go.
CHORUS
2ND TENOR.
cresc.
Dig-gy dad-dy, hear him weep, Dig-gy dad-dy, hear him sigh.
1ST TENOR & 1st BASS.
Diggy daddy hear him weep, O! Diggy daddy hear him
2ND BASS.
f
'way down the Ca - ri - o, And the old man kicky up and zig zag jig jag, die.
1st
2nd
kicky up and jig jag, kicky up and die.
sigh,
zig zag jig jag, die.

'way down the Ca - ri - o, O! . . And the old man kicky up and zig zag jig jag, die.

4. It follered her to jail one day, for Mary she drank rum,—
Now's her chance to pare that corn for thirty days to come.

5. Old Abram's charming daughter bold, sweet "Mamie of the Vale,"
Along with old Bob Ridley playing teeter on a rail.

6. The old man's got a bull-dog fierce, his daughter she is fine,
† His boots are on, his bull-dog loose at a quarter after nine.

* Groaning. † Some MSS. read "He turns the gas and the bulldog out at a quarter after nine."

CHORAL MARCH. *

With spirit.

V. E. BECKER.

On, gal - lant com - pa - ny, with mea-sured step and song; While cheer-ful
songs re - sound, the way is ne - ver long. La la la la la la la la
Left, right, strict in time,
la Left, right, strict in time,
Firm step, close in line,
la la la la la la Straight a - head, nought shall stay Our tri - um-phant
Firm step, close in line,
la la la la la la, Left, right, strict in time, Firm step, close in line,
way; On! La la la la la la la la la la la la
Left, right, strict in time, Firm step, close in line,
Love,
straight a - head, nought shall stay our glor - - ious way. Tra ta ra ta. La la
joy.... and.... mu - - - sic, In - - - vite.... us.... on..........
la la la la la la la la la la la la
Love, joy, and mu - - - sic, In -

* By permission of Edwin Ashdown, Hanover Sq., London.

ward
la la. Thus in jol-ly com-pa-ny, Wan-der we, light and free, Mak-ing, as we
vite us.
FINE.
roam, Each rest-ing-place our home, As we roam, As we roam, As we roam, Ev'ry place our home.
TRIO.
Schrum, schrum, schrum, schrum, When we wea-ry are at night, Beams the cheerful
la la la la la la la la
hos-tel light, Quick-ly in, For with-in Good-ly cheer a-waits;.....
la la la la la la la la la la
Pret-ty maidens whom we meet, Gal-lant-ly we al-ways greet; Ere we part,
la la la la la la la la la la la la
1st
2nd
Many a heart Owns their gen-tle sway. Yes, sway Hol-la ho! Hol-la
Hol-la ho!

ho! We're light and free where'er we go, Hol-la ho! hol-la ho! We're
Hol-la ho! hol-la ho! hol-la ho!
light and free where'er we go; Love and joy and mu - - - - - -
Love and joy and mu - - sic,
sic are beck' - - - - ning us on - - - ward,.......
all in-vite us on - - ward, all in-vite us on - - ward. Yes, 'tis
Love and joy and mu - - - sic.......... all in-vite us
glad - some mu - - sic,
on - - ward, la la la la la la la la la la la la la la la la la
DA CAPO SENZA REPLICA
1st
2nd
la la la la la la la la la la la la la la la la, Hol-la la la la.

OLD VOICES.

"**The past never comes back**; our fancies are **but the ideal** ghosts of things that were."
—PROF. G. P. YOUNG.

Words by W. W. CAMPBELL, '85.
ARTHUR E. FISHER.
Andante, quasi recitativo.
VOICE
PIANO
I stand on the confines of the
past to-night, The world that is gone be - fore, And in the soft flicker of the fire's dim light, Old
shadows steal be-fore my sight, From its strange and mis - ty shore. And
piu mosso.
by - - gone murmurs are in my ears, And sweet lips touch my cheeks, ... And

accel. e cresc.
old, old tunes that no one hears, That steal to me from the sad old years. And
dim.
sweet words that no one speaks.
dim.
f
sf
p
quasi recitativo
p
But on-ly the rhythm of an old time tune, That steals down the halls of
p
pp
ppp
time; And comes so soft like the far off rune Of a stream that sleeps thro' the afternoon, Or a

mf. più mosso
dis - tant evening chime.. And in the si-lence that
mf.
in - ter - venes, Sad voi - ces whis - per low; "Come back once more to the
p
f
accel. e cresc.
loved old scenes. To the dim old regions of boy-hood's dreams, The sweet world you used to
accel. e cresc.
sf.
know, the sweet world.... you used.... to know."..................
sf
sf.
p

ENVOY.

Words by H. ST.Q. CAYLEY, '81.
J. EDMUND JONES, '88.
Andante.
Voice.
Piano.
Three-score and ten, a wise man said, were our years to be:
Three-score and six I give him back,.......... Four are enough for me.
Four in these cor - ri-dors, Four in these halls of ours, These give me
Heav'n-ly Pow'rs, 'Tis life for me. me.
cresc.
1st
2nd

INDEX TO TITLES.

	PAGE
A la Claire Fontaine	10
Alma Mater	47
Alma Mater	90
Alouette	55
Amo, Amas, I Love a Lass	54
A-Roving	56
Auf Wiedersehn	124
Auld Lang Syne	94
Aura Lee	120
Austrian National Hymn	19
Away, Away, Away	120
Bagpipes, The	83
Bonnie Doon	94
Boots, The	59
Breathe Soft, Ye Winds	162
Bridget Donaghue	139
Brigadier, Le	24
Broken Ring, The	123
Bull Dog, The	74
—Camping Song	104
Canada, the Gem in the Crown	3
Canadian Boat Song, A	114
Capital Ship, A	112
Carmen Liberorum Romanorum	68
Chinese Song	84
Choral March	167
Cloud Cap't Towers, The	143
College Gown, The	73
Commencement	90
Cruise of the Bugaboo, The	28
Dear Evelina	51
Der Wirthin Töchterlein	66
Diggy, Daddy, Hear Him Weep	166
Drapeau de Carillon, Le	164
Drink to Me Only	114
Dulce Domum	67
En Roulant ma Boule	138
Envoy	173
Eulalie	129
Farewell	163
Farewell to the Forest	130
Forsaken am I	121
Forty Years On	31
Freshman's Fate, The	38
Gaudeamus Igitur	80
Glory and Love to the Men of Old. (Faust)	153
God Preserve our Native Land	2
God Save the Queen	2
Good Night, Ladies	75
Good Night. (Round)	66
Hail, Columbia	15
Halli-Hallo	140
Heigho, Heigho	72
Here's to the Maiden	118
Home by the Sea, A	125
Honour Old 'Varsity	89
$H_2 S O_4$	43
Integer Vitae	62
I'se Gwine Back to Dixie	122
I've Lost my Doggy	127
Jingle, Bells	36
Johnny Schmoker	116
Juanita	152
Kemo Kimo	33
Kermesse Scene. (Faust)	145
Kingdom Coming	100
Landlady's Daughter, The	66
Litoria	22
Litoria. (Freshman's Version)	23
Lorelei, Die	96
Maid from Algoma, The	23
Maid from Algoma, The. (Second Version)	24
Malbrouck	88
Maple Leaf For Ever, The	7
Marching Song	73
March of the Men of Harlech	14
Marseillaise, La	16
Massa's in the Cold Ground	110
May God Preserve Thee, Canada	1
Meerschaum Pipe	62
Mermaid, The	85
Merrily, Merrily. (Round)	75
Michael Roy	52
Minstrel Boy, The	13
Mush, Mush	30
My Bonnie	45
Oh, my Darling Clementine	44
O'Hooliban	35
Old Black Joe	97
Old Folks at Home	103
Old Grimes	21
Old Voices	170
On the Banks of the Yang-tsee-kiang	142
O Tempora, O Mores	27
Our Irish Bedel	26
Our New Degree	82
Peggy Murphy	78
Peter Gray	50
Pipe, The	58
Poachers of Lincolnshire, The	102
Polly Wolly Doodle	41
Pork, Beans and Hard Tack	78

	PAGE
Regimental Song of the Queen's Own Rifles	68
Revelry of the Dying	119
Rosalie	98
Row Your Boat. (Round)	43
Rule, Britannia	11
Russian National Anthem	20
Sailing Across the Sea	160
Sailing, Sailing, Sailing	42
Sail, Sail, My Bark Canoe	91
Saw, My Leg Off	83
Scots Wha Hae	13
Seeing Nellie Home	40
Sleep, Lady, Sleep	150
Sleighrider's Serenade	128
Soldier's Farewell	117
Solomon Levi	76
Son of a Gambolier	64
Spanish Guitar, The	48
Speed Away	131
Stars of the Summer Night	137
Stars of the Summer Night (as sung at Yale)	137
Stars Trembling o'er Us	115
Still Night, The. (A Catch)	133
Tale of Two Idles, A	49
Tarpaulin Jacket, The	92
Temperance Corps, The	132
Tenting on the Old Camp Ground	95
There is a Tavern in the Town	38
There's Only Room for One	61
Those Evening Bells	70
Three Crows, The	71
Three Little Kittens	70
Tramp's Song, The	34
Treue Liebe	134
Two Roses, The	101
Ubi Bene, Ibi Patria	46
Un Canadien Errant	9
Undergraduate's Lament, The	57
Upidee. (Yale Version)	86
Vicar of Bray, The	106
Vive la Canadienne	9
Vive la Compagnie	81
Wacht am Rhein, Die	18
'Way up on the Mountain-Top-tip-top	87
Ye Shepherds Tell Me	134
Young Recruit, The	107

INDEX TO FIRST LINES.

	PAGE.
A capital ship for an ocean trip	112
Ach! wie ist's möglich dann	134
Ah! can it truly be	134
Airily float we with gentle swing	120
A la claire fontaine	10
Allons, enfants de la patrie	16
All the world around I'm straying	46
Alouette, gentille Alouette	55
Amo, Amas, I love a lass	54
And are they done, those halcyon days	90
An exile lone and sad	9
As I was walking down the street	72
As the blackbird, in the spring	120
A tall, stalwart lancer lay dying	92
At number three, Old England Square	56
A voice resounds like thunder peal	18
Away down south in Centre street	33
Breathe soft, ye winds	162
Bring hither a beaker and fill it with wine	81
Canada, the Star and Dominion	3
Come all ye tender-hearted men	28
Come listen to our hearty song	73
Come youths and maidens all	38
Comrades, brothers in the battle	90
Concinamus, O sodales	67
Dashing through the snow	36
Deux gendarmes, un beau dimanche	24
Drink to me only with thine eyes	114
Ene mene mine mo	68
En roulant ma boule roulant	138
Es braust ein Ruf wie Donnerhall	18
Es ist bestimmt in Gottes Rath	124
Es zogen drei Bursche wohl über den Rhein	66
Faintly as tolls the evening chime	114
Far in a shaded valley	123
Forsaken am I	121
Forty years on, when afar and asunder	31
Gaudeamus igitur	80
Glory and love to the men of old	153
God preserve our native land	2
God preserve our noble sov'reign	19
God save our gracious Queen	2
Gone are the days when my heart was young	97
Good night	66
Good night, ladies	75
Gott erhalte Franz den Kaiser	19
Hail Columbia, happy land	15
Hark! I hear a voice	87
Here's to the maiden of bashful fifteen	118
How can I bear to leave thee	117
Ich weiss nicht was soll es bedeuten	96
I'm a rambling rake of poverty	64
Im Wald und auf der Haide	140
In a cabin, in a canon	44
In Brooklyn city there lived a maid	52
In days of yore from Britain's shore	7
In einem kühlen Grunde	123
In every land, by God's command	124
In good King Charles' golden days	106
Integer vitae scelerisque purus	62
In the sky the bright stars glittered	40
I'se gwine back to Dixie	122
I stand on the confines of the past to-night	170
It was in the County Kerry	139
I've lost my doggie	127
Je suis Pierre le bon-ton de Paris	98
Johnny Schmoker	116
Long live our noble Czar	20
Malbrouck s'en va-t-en guerre	88
May God preserve thee, Canada	1
Me gettee married	84
Me name it is O'Hoolihan	35
Men of Harlech! in the hollow	14
Merrily, merrily, greet the morn	75
Minstrel awaken the harp from its slumbers	89
Morgen muss ich fort von hier	163
My Bonnie is over the ocean	45
My name is Polly Hill	142
My name is Solomon Levi	76
Now we'll sing you a tale of two idles	49
O Carillon! je te revois encore	164
O Carillon! to thee once more returning	164
Of all things on earth that to joy give birth	58
Oft in the classic page I've read	73
Oft in the stilly night	133
Oh! Alma Mater, thus I think, and then I sigh	47
Oh! give me a home by the sea	125
O hills, O vales of pleasure	130
Oh! I went down south for to see my Sal	41
Oh! swate Peggy Murphy had beautiful eyes	78
Oh! tell me what it meaneth	96
Oh! the bull-dog on the bank	74
Oh! 'twas there I larned radin' and writin'	30
Oh! who will smoke my meerschaum pipe	62
Old Grimes is dead, that good old man	21
Ole massa bought a bran new coat	166
On a bank two roses fair	101
On a painted ocean a painted ship	160
Once on a time there lived a man	50
Once on a time there were three little kittens	70
On, gallant company, with measured step and song	167
Our volunteers are soldiers bold	78
Over the river, over the Dee	42

	PAGE.
Red or white liquor, coarse or fine	145
Round de meadows am a-ringing	110
Row, row, row, your boat	43
Saw my leg off	83
Say, arkeys, hab you seen de massa	100
Scots wha hae wi' Wallace bled	13
See these ribbons gaily streaming	107
Should auld acquaintance be forgot	94
Sleep, lady, sleep	150
Soft o'er the fountain	152
Some spake of O'Connell, the great Liberator	26
Speed away on thine errand of light	131
Star of the summer eve	129
Stars of the summer night	137
Stars of the summer night. (As sung at Yale)	137
Stars trembling o'er us	115
The cloud-cap't towers, the gorgeous palaces	143
The festal day has come	59
The king of the north has clothed the earth	128
The minstrel boy to the war is gone	13
There is a tavern in the town	38
There's only room for one	61
There was a jolly fiddler	27
There were three crows sat on a tree	71
The shades of night were comin' down swift	86
Those evening bells, those evening bells	70
Three score and ten, a wise man	173
Three students that came from far over the Rhine	66
Through wood and forest ranging	140

	PAGE.
To Chancellor and Senate, too	57
'Twas at our last college dinner	82
'Twas Friday morn when we set sail	85
Un Canadien errant	9
Up, comrades, up! 'tis our bugle	68
Vive la Canadienne	9
'Way down in the meadow	51
'Way down in yonder valley	34
'Way down upon the Swanee ribber	103
We have left far behind us the dwellings of men	104
We meet 'neath the sounding rafter	119
We're tenting to-night on the old camp ground	95
We're the temp'rance corps of the Q. O. R.	132
When Britain first at Heaven's command	11
When I was a student at Cadiz	48
When I was bound apprentice	102
When the golden dawn of day	163
Where are you going, my pretty maid?	23
Where are you going, my pretty maid? (2nd vers'n)	24
Where the pine tree waveth	91
Ye banks and braes of bonnie Doon	94
Ye blooming freshman dons his gown	22
Ye shepherds, tell me have you seen	134
Ye sons of France, awake to glory	16
Ye 'Varsity man has doffed his gown	23
Yi, yi, yi, yi	83
You take a few pieces of zinc	43

*** As a great deal of the music of this book is printed with vocal parts only, it will be specially noted that in many cases the upper stave is to be played an octave lower than it is written.

Committee of Compilation and Management.

J. E. Jones, '88, - - - *Chairman.*

J. D. Spence, '89, - - - *Secretary.* | N. Kent, '88, - - - *Treasurer.*

M. S. Mercer, '85.	J. W. Garvin, '87.
R. M. Hamilton, '87.	W. J. Healy, '88.
R. L. Johnston, '87.	F. B. Hodgins, '88.
A. H. Young, '87.	J. J. Ferguson, '90.

MUSIC PRIMERS.

EDITED BY DR. STAINER.

In issuing this series of Music Primers the editor sees with pleasure the realization of a desire that has long been felt, to place in the hands of teachers and students of music a set of educational works of a high standard at a price so low as to render them attainable by all.

The growing interest in music generally, and rapid spread of its study, so very evident in this country, render it of the utmost importance that the student's first steps in every branch should be directed with skill and based on sound principles. The Editor has kept this object steadily in view, and he believes that each one of these Primers will prove to be as carefully constructed in detail as it is comprehensive in design.

Such a result would have been impossible but for the hearty support and sympathy of those authors, men of known ability in their special branches of art, who have embodied the results of their long and valuable experience in their respective contributions.

While gratefully acknowledging the kindness of these gentlemen, the Editor cannot but express a hope that the Primers may prove as useful to the public, and as beneficial to art, as both authors and publishers have endeavoured to make them.

MISCELLANEOUS PART SONGS.

FOR MIXED VOICES.

Cents.

1 Dulce Domum. S. A. T. B., G. A. Macfarren 05

2 Down among the dead men. S. A. T. B., G. A. Macfarren 05

3 The girl I've left behind me. S. A. T. B., G. A. Macfarren 05

4 British Grenadiers. S. A. T. B., G. A. Macfarren 08

5 Long live England's future Queen. S.A.T.B, Dr. Rimbault 08

6 My task is ended (Song and Chorus). A. T. B. B. Balfe 12

7 Thus spake one summer's day. S.A.T.B., Abt 08

8 Soldiers' Chorus Gounod 12

9 The Kermesse Scene (from "Faust") " 15

10 Up, quit thy bower. S.A.T.B. Brinley Richards 12

11 Maidens, never go a-wooing. S.S.T.T.B. G. A. Macfarren 08

12 Faggot Binders' Chorus Gounod 12

13 Sylvan Hours (for six female voices) Joseph Robinson 15

14 The Gipsy Chorus. T.T.B.B. Balfe 12

15 Ave Maria Arcadelt 05

16 Hark! the herald angels sing. S.A.T.B. Mendelssohn 05

17 England yet (Solo and Chorus). S.A.T.B. Jules Benedict 08

18 The Shepherd's Sabbath Day. S.A.T.B. J. L. Hatton 08

19 Thoughts of Childhood. S.A.T.B. Henry Smart 08

20 Spring's Return. S.A.T.B. " " 08

21 An old Church Song. S.A.T.B. " " 08

22 Sabbath Bells. S.A.T.B. " " 08

23 Serenade. S.A.T.B. " " 08

24 Cold Autumn Wind. S.A.T.B. " " 08

25 Orpheus with his lute. S.S.S. Bennett Gilbert 08

26 Lullaby. S.A.A. " " 05

27 This is my own, my native land. S.A.T.B. G. A. Macfarren 05

28 March of the Men of Harlech. S.A.T.B. Dr. Rimbault 08

29 God Save the Queen. S.A.T.B. Dr. Rimbault 05

30 Rule, Britannia. S.A.T.B " " 05

31 The Retreat. T.T.B.B. L. de Rille 08

32 Lo! morn is breaking. S.S.S. Cherubini 08

33 We are Spirits. S.S.S. G. A. Macfarren 12

34 Market Chorus (Masaniello). S.A.T.B. Auber 12

35 The Prayer (Masaniello). S.A.T.B. " 05

36 The Water Sprites. S.A.T.B. Kücken 08

37 Eve's glittering star. S.A.T.B. " 08

38 When first the primrose. S.A.T.B. " 08

39 O dewdrop bright. S.A.T.B. " 05

40 Sanctus, from the "Messe Solenelle." S.A.T.B. Rossini 12

41 Nine Kyries, Ancient and Modern Rossini 08

42 Sun of my soul. S.A.T.B. Brinley Richards 08

43 'Twas fancy and the ocean's spray. S.A.T.B. G. A. Osborne 08

44 A Prayer for those at Sea. S.A.T.B. G. A. Osborne 08

45 O Thou whose power (Prayer from "Mose in Egitto") Rossini 08

46 The Guard on the Rhine. S.A.T.B. G. A. Macfarren 05

47 The German Fatherland. S.A.T.B. G. A. Macfarren 05

48 The Lord is my Shepherd (Quartet). S.A.T.B G. A. Osborne 08

49 Te Deum, in F Jackson 08

50 Te Deum, in F Nares 08

51 Charity (La Carita). S.S.S. Rossini 12

52 Cordelia. A.T.T.B. G. A. Osborne 12

53 I know. S.A.T.B. Walter Hay 08

54 Chorus of Handmaidens (from "Fridolin") A. Randegger 12

55 The Offertory Sentences Edmund Rogers 12

56 The Red Cross Knight Dr. Calcott 08

57 The Chough and Crow Sir H. R. Bishop 10

58 The "Carnovale." Rossini 08

59 Softly falls the moonlight Edmund Rogers 12

60 Air of Himmel Henry Leslie 08

61 Offertory Sentences E. Sauerbrey 12

62 The Ressurection C. Villiers Stanford 15

63 Our Boys. New Patriotic Song. H. J. Byron and W. M. Lutz 12

64 The Men of Wales Brinley Richards 08

65 Dame Durden 05

66 A little farm well tilled Hook 05

67 There was a simple maiden G. A. Macfarren 05

68 Fair Hebe G. A. Macfarren 05

69 Once I loved a maiden fair G. A. Macfarren 05

70 The joval man of Kent G. A. Macfarren 05

71 The oak and the ash G. A. Macfarren 05

72 Heart of Oak. G. A. Macfarren 05

73 Come to the sunset Tree W. A. Philpott 12

74 May S.A.T.B. W. F. Banks 08

75 Pure, lovely innocence. "Il Re di Labore." Chorus for Female voices G. Massenet 12

76 A Love Idyl. S.A.T.B. E. R. Terry 08

77 Hail to the Woods! A.T.T.B. J. Yarwood 08

78 Near the town of Taunton Dean Dudeney 08

79 Our merry boys at sea Yarwood 08

80 The shepherd's Farewell Berlioz 10

81 When the sun sets o'er the mountains ("Il Demonio.") A. Rubinstein 10

82 Hymn of Nature Beethoven 10

83 Michaelmas Day. (Humorous Part Songs, No. 1.) Walter Maynard 12

84 Sporting Notes. (Humorous Part Songs, No. 2.). Walter Maynard 12

85 Austrian National Hymn Haydn 12

86 A May Carol. S.S.C. Joseph Robinson 12

87 The bright-hair'd Morn is glowing. S.A.T.B. Theodor L. Clemens 10

88 Oh Rest. ("Valleda.") C. H. Lenepveu 12

89 Love reigneth over all. T.T.B.B. C. G. Elsasser 15

90 Joy Waltz. T.T.B.B. C. G. Elsasser 15

91 The Star of Bethlehem. (Christmas Carol.) Theodor L. Clemens 08

92 Busy, Curious, Thirsty Fly. T.A.T.B. Theodor L. Clemens 10

93 Love Wakes and Weeps. A.T.B.B. Felix W. Morley 08

www.ingramcontent.com/pod-product-compliance
Lightning Source LLC
Chambersburg PA
CBHW020535270326
41927CB00006B/590

* 9 7 8 3 3 3 7 1 8 1 2 8 4 *